COMMON THINGS
UNCOMMON
WAYS

Sunny Kobe Cook

Achievement Dynamics, Inc.
Publishers of Self-Education and Personal Achievement Works

Common Things Uncommon Ways

Published by Achievement Dynamics, Inc.
Publishers of Self-Education and Personal Achievement Works.

Printed and manufactured in the United States

ISBN: 0-9662120-3-7

To my loving husband, John Murphy
for his unending support, encouragement and love
not just on this project, but every day.
Thank you for pushing the dark clouds away
so that I could once again bask in the sun.

To my two greatest mentors,
Garry Coats and Ted Shepherd.
So much of what I know I learned
from watching the two of you.
Thank you for leading by such great examples.

And to my lifelong friend, Robert Olsen
my deepest gratitude for never
letting me forget my dream.
"Who else but a bosom buddy . . . "

Acknowledgement

Over the years, I've had the privilege of knowing and working with countless talented, dedicated people. Many of their examples are included in these pages. Stories have been retold and conversations recounted as accurately as my memory allows. It is my intention to honor each of them by sharing their collective wisdom through this book.

Thank you for the inspiration. I hope many will benefit from your contributions.

CONTENTS

About the Title

*"When you do the common things in life
in an uncommon way, you will command
the attention of the world."*
— George Washington Carver

I ran across this quote in a magazine when I was still in high school and posted a copy on my locker door. Later, I pasted it on my refrigerator. I embraced the sentiment and it became the words I chose to live by. The simple, underlying message of honor in doing even the most menial task or job well echoed my upbringing. I can't begin to count the number of times I heard my father say, "I don't care if you are the garbage collector, just be the best darn garbage collector anyone has ever seen."

Throughout my working life, I have strived to be "uncommon," to leave my mark on tasks, jobs, companies and industries. I have also had the privilege of working with many others who were "uncommon." I salute them and all those who will follow in their footsteps.

INTRODUCTION

Whipping Up Your Own Secret Sauce

Have you ever really thought about what makes a business successful? Do you find yourself reading articles about companies, looking for their "secret sauce?" When you see a booming business, do you wonder how it accomplished its success? Would you like to find a "secret formula" for your own business? Even if you aren't a business owner, would you benefit from improving the success of your team?

Some businesses become successful through unique products alone. If you happen to have the next hula-hoop or Pokemon in your hands, don't bother reading this now. Your window of opportunity is historically brief — come back when your fad has faded!

More companies achieve success as a result of innovative marketing strategies. Often, these companies do *common things*. Nike makes athletic shoes. McDonald's sells hamburgers. Coca-Cola and Pepsi brew soft drinks. Starbucks pours coffee. Southwest Airlines flies passengers from point A to point B. Sleep Country USA sells mattresses. The list is endless.

None of those products would be considered unique. Quite the contrary - they are common things. Yet all of these businesses found ways to not only be successful, but also grow into industry and profit leaders by doing *"common things"* in *"uncommon ways."*

When I analyze successful businesses, I find many different variables, but I also notice significant similarities. I believe *all* successful businesses share one basic trait. Regardless of the industry or commodities in which they trade, they recognize and maximize their single greatest resource - ***their people***. A company's success is a combination of the success of its individuals.

You may not sell mattresses or even be in retail, but here's some good news - the principles of building successful businesses through employee motivation are not industry specific. They do not require a recognized spokesperson or an advertising budget equal to the national debt. They are transferable to virtually any business concept.

Even better, you don't even have to own your own business to implement these proven techniques in your organization. You can put these techniques to work *today* if you fill any management or team leader role.

Some people believe if enough dollars are spent in advertising, success will follow. To a degree, that is true. An aggressive advertising campaign can cement your brand name and jingle in the consumers' mind and in doing so, earn your company unprecedented market share. Now, I apologize to anyone annoyed by seemingly endless ads, but we must recognize that advertising is a necessary "evil" for any business. Advertising dollars pay for the free television you watch and subsidize the cost of everything from sporting event tickets to live entertainment to public transportation.

Advertising is at least partially responsible for the success of most businesses. I won't attempt to sort out how much you should advertise, or what forum is right for your business, but I will assure you advertising alone will not make your business successful. All advertising does is bring customers through your door. What happens once they cross your threshold, if and what they buy, if they return and if they tell their friends, is the direct result of their experience with your employees.

Whether you own your own business, a manager in a large conglomerate, or somewhere in between, the true "secret to success" rests not in *your* hands, but in the hands *your employees.*

I learned this principle as a secretary in a sales office for an international company. The only way to get noticed and promoted was to build a stellar team. Working in retail, I soon realized it didn't matter how many customers advertising brought through the door. Whether or not they became customers depended on how they were treated in the store. As an entrepreneur, I quickly learned my investment, dream and reputation did not rest solely in my hands, but rather in the hands of every member of my staff.

In these pages, we will explore some of the many ways to motivate these precious individuals who can take your team, organization or company to new heights of performance, profitability and customer satisfaction.

To begin, I will clarify what I believe your role should be once you accept a management position.

Then I will discuss what truly motivates employees. Good news – it's NOT money. Recognition, a sense of contribution and a sense of belonging all rate higher than money. I'll spend a lot of time on recognition, not only because it consistently ranks number one, but also because it lays the foundation for the next two highest ranked employee motivators. If you simply attempt to create a sense of contribution and belonging for employees without first giving them recognition, your results won't be as significant. Not only are there countless ways to give recognition, how you give it is also important so we'll discuss it in depth.

In the chapters detailing each employee motivator, I will offer practical, inexpensive ways to implement these principles.

My examples are great ideas I've borrowed from every manager and company I've worked for along with some of my own. Each one was tested and proven successful in a real business.

This management style is not only "employee friendly," it improves your bottom line while building customer loyalty.

People often mistakenly assume some of the ideas I've implemented bear earmarks of a woman-owned business. Occasionally, my husband affectionately calls some of my ways of thinking "chick logic." Admittedly, I am a woman and do some things differently as a result.

However, I must confess, I have never worked for a female boss. All I learned and put to use in my career came from great men who were inspiring leaders. The principles are not gender specific.

The ideas in this book don't have to be used exactly as described. Once you understand the premise, you can add your own personal touches, adapt ideas to your business and make them your own. And if you've already developed other great ways to motivate employees, I hope you'll share. You can contact me through my website www.SunnyKobeCook.com.

The last chapter, "Leading with your Heart" sums everything up. I firmly believe the secret to success – in life and business – is to do just that. I hope these pages will offer you insights, ideas and inspiration as you strive to do common things in uncommon ways.

CHAPTER ONE

Drafting Your Own Dream Team

O ne day your business suddenly grows beyond your own garage. You find you can no longer answer every telephone call, pay every invoice, handle every sale and deliver every piece of inventory or service personally. You are ready to hire your first employee. Your obvious success brings with it new challenges.

Instead of performing detailed tasks, you are now called on to build a team of people who **will** answer your telephone, pay invoices, sell merchandise and make deliveries. Your role has now changed and many entrepreneurs and new managers find themselves unprepared for the shift.

By nature, most small businesses require owners to wear many hats. Often, financial constraints force us to "do it all." As the business grows, we hire employees because we have more tasks than we can manage alone. Most likely, we haven't given much thought to our changing role in this new and growing organization. We are too busy just trying to get the work done!

However, before we hire, we first need to critically analyze our individual strengths and weaknesses. Yes, I'm aware you know how to do every task in the business and that you've been doing them – or at least the essential ones – for some time. But what are your unique talents and skills? Where might your time be best spent?

Some entrepreneurs are great salespeople, but struggle to maintain the books. Some are detail-oriented and others stockpile government, tax or insurance forms and papers in the back of a drawer. None of these characteristics alone are indicators of success or impending doom, but they are important facts to know about yourself before you begin hiring staff and delegating tasks.

One of my friends owns a very successful sales training company based in Atlanta. He became frustrated after a few years of growth. He knew he had to add more people to allow the company to grow to its full potential, but he didn't know exactly what roles they should play. So he took advantage of the perspectives of his current employees to identify the company's weaknesses.

He did a survey and asked each person to list his or her strengths and unique talents. Assuring them everyone has them, he then asked them to list their greatest weaknesses. What did they like most about their jobs? What did they like least? Then he took it a step further and asked them to do the same candid review of him. They were allowed to do that particular analysis anonymously, if preferred.

Using this survey, he found areas where technology could improve performance, as well as job satisfaction. He saw tasks that could be realigned within a department to take advantage of individuals' skills and preferences. In addition, he not only found the weaknesses he needed to fill, but also discovered that others would welcome tasks and responsibilities he had been handling.

Once you've assessed your individual strengths, look at the list of essential tasks that must be performed. Which fall in the areas of your greatest weaknesses? Hire someone for those areas first! Do this review each and every time you consider hiring a new person and you will hire not only the right person for the job, but also the right person to help your company grow to the next level.

If you continually hire to fill your weaknesses or the weaknesses of your organization, you will find it easier to delegate. You'll readily hand over the tasks and responsibilities you know can be handled more effectively by someone else. You will also likely breathe a sigh of relief and sleep a little better at night knowing employees who actually enjoy these areas are managing these details more efficiently.

That is the first secret to building an unbeatable team. Find people who excel in areas where you don't, give them tasks as well as responsibility and then let them go for it! If, as your company grows, you gradually find your employees need you less and less on a daily basis, congratulations! You are doing it right!

Big corporations also share this challenge. In this age of "downsizing" and "rightsizing," we continually ask those around us to do more with less. The good news is the formula is the same whether you own the company or manage a group of any size for someone else.

Maybe you've just been named a team leader, department head, supervisor, assistant manager or even manager. You may now carry the title of editor, controller, vice-president, president or any combination of letters following "C," such as CEO, CFO, COO. All of these titles, however you prefer to think of them, share a common description in the unwritten business dictionary.

n. "One who is judged by
the performance of others."

The best professional salespeople often pride themselves on only being concerned with their own performances and being their own bosses. Yet even they will likely agree others play a role in their successes. It may be the administrative person who makes sure their telephone calls get through to the decision maker, or someone in their own company who helps execute an order on a timely basis. For virtually all of us, working with others is an essential skill necessary to our success. But few of us are formally trained in this area.

This is equally true of managers. In fact, people often move into management positions without much training in what they actually manage – people! When we find ourselves unprepared for our new management positions, we typically react one of two ways. We either continue to act as we always have, doing our jobs exactly the same way, trying our best to ignore the new title; or we retreat into our new offices and begin barking orders, determined to "whip this place into shape." Both methods are guaranteed to ultimately fail.

What we really need is to embrace a new leadership-oriented mindset, one that will help us make the tough decisions required of us in our new roles as managers or employers.

Making tough calls: hiring and firing

Everyone I know agrees hiring decisions are among the hardest to make. Some great interviewees don't work out, while others who don't interview as well prove to be genuine assets to your company. There are shelves full of books offering probing questions to help you fine tune your interviewing skills, and I don't profess mine to be without fail, so you'll have to find your own path down that particular road.

What I will offer are a few bits of collective wisdom from great hiring managers I've known. First, trust your gut. Animals trust their flight instincts, but we humans discount ours too often. If something doesn't ring true about an applicant, there's probably a good reason. You're better off passing.

The relationship you are looking to forge is one of complete trust – you are about to put the reputation of your business in this person's hands. If something about them nags you, you will never completely trust them and one day, you will learn why you had those doubts in the first place. And who knows what fallout there may be within your organization by the time you realize you should have trusted your instincts?

Second, look for attitude over skill. That is not to say a perky personality makes up for a complete lack of accounting skills in a controller. However, it is possible to find pleasant people who are good at their jobs. Unhappy people are easy to spot. You don't have to be a master at reading body language to pick them out.

The best way is to observe them when they don't realize they're being watched. No, I'm not advocating "Big Brother" tactics with hidden cameras. There are easier, less offensive ways to accomplish this goal.

As a matter of practice, applicants should be in your lobby or customer waiting area for at least 10 minutes. This is not to be rude, it's to see how they make use of their time. Let your receptionist in on the game and let him or her play a vital role in your hiring process. Later, you will learn other reasons this is important, but for now, let's stick to the obvious. Who is in a better position to observe applicants unobtrusively? Who better to give you a snapshot of them during unguarded moments?

After you escort interviewees into your office, excuse yourself for a moment and confer privately with your "front office eyes and ears." Were they pleasant? Did they make small talk with the receptionist or did they "talk down" to them? Did they ask questions about the company? What sort of questions? (By the way, "When is the next paid holiday?" would **not** be the ideal question for applicants to ask.) If you display company materials in the lobby, did they read them? Look at them? Show any interest in them? All these bits of information will give you a glimpse into the "non-interview" personalities of the people you are considering.

Once you've established this role with your "front office eyes and ears," the conversation between you and your staffer will become very brief. The information gleaned from those 10 minutes waiting in your reception area will prove invaluable.

One of my bosses used to have me escort prospective applicants down the maze of hallways from the lobby to his office. Along the way, I chatted with the candidates. I found these unguarded moments visiting with "a secretary" to be revealing.

Communication between the manager and I evolved into a simple bit of sign language. I showed them in and while closing the door offered a discreet "thumbs up" or "thumbs down." This simple indicator of whether or not I spotted any red flags during our walk/talk proved uncannily accurate. We would then get together after the applicant left and I would explain the reasoning behind my "vote." Rarely did our opinions vary.

In fact, the only applicant who got a "thumbs down" from me and still got the job proved to be a disastrous employee. However, he did provide many years of amusement for us all as we retold stories of his antics, and for years he upheld my reputation for never making inaccurate calls. Of course, once I had to make hiring decisions on a larger scale, my batting average became more reflective of the norm.

Lastly, *always, always, always* call references. If

you can, get home telephone numbers of supervisors from the candidate's last few positions. If the applicant left on good terms, they may have that information and permission to share it. People are often much more candid outside coworkers' earshot. If they don't have this personal information, call them at work. Just be sure you aren't trapped into just accepting the Human Resources recording, "Yes, he or she worked here from this date to that."

Even if direct supervisors, constrained by company policy, can only give you bare facts, plus whether or not the candidate is eligible for rehire, they will convey a lot with their inflection and overall demeanor at the mention of the person's name. This is the equivalent of a passing motorist flashing their lights to alert you to a speed trap ahead. It may only be a flicker, but it's a warning you'll be wise to heed.

It may seem fatalistic to talk about hiring and firing on the same page, but the truth is sometimes, despite our best efforts, we do not make good hiring decisions. Everyone I know has made at least one mistake. The real tragedy comes not from the error in judgment, but from the failure to promptly rectify the situation once it becomes obvious. Again, there are many sources you can turn to for information about whether you are being too hasty. This is not one of them.

Every company I have been associated with had

very low turnover once employees passed probationary periods. They also had average to high turnover during those initial weeks or months when managers were evaluating their hiring decisions. In all fairness, I should also mention they all had extraordinarily high performance teams that set records in their companies and industries.

So yes, it is sometimes not only necessary – but critical – to fire someone. It is not easy or pleasant, but it really is to everyone's benefit. Unhappy, unproductive people who don't fit the culture of your organization bring the entire group down. Sour attitudes sour your entire team and worse, reflect poorly on you as a leader. By the time you know you made a bad hiring decision, everyone else in the office already knows it. In fact, they're probably wondering when you are going to get a clue and do something about it!

You may think you're being fair and kind by not swinging the ax swiftly, but what you are really doing is keeping this person from finding a position or company where their strengths and talents will be appreciated. Worse still, you are telling your team this sort of attitude and performance is acceptable. Lowering standards is a slippery slope you must avoid at all costs if you want to be successful over the long haul.

Every dream team needs a coach

Now that you've built the right team, you must motivate these high performance individuals to reach their fullest potential. They are now valuable resources you can use to solve problems for both the company and customers. You need to insure they are dedicated to the company, customers and excellence.

No matter how great a team you build, there is one role the owner or manager cannot and should not ever delegate – leader. In my opinion, "leader" is just short for your full title, "Company Cheerleader." Your permanent, ongoing responsibility is to motivate those individuals who hold the reputation of your business in their hands.

Once you've accepted your new challenge, you will realize your role has indeed changed. You are now no longer focused on serving your external consumers, but rather the many internal consumers within your organization.

Before you can successfully devise a plan to motivate your employees, you must first understand what really motivates people. Take some guesses.

If **money** is the first thing that comes to mind, you're not alone. I've posed this question to numerous business groups I've spoken to over the years, and money is the most common response.

You might be surprised to learn, however, that once basic needs are met, money quickly drops to number **four** on the list of employee motivations. Managers who throw **money** at every situation are no doubt wasting resources, maybe even with lackluster results.

Every survey I've ever seen lists some variation of these three answers as the top employee motivators: recognition; contribution and belonging. The best news – all of these "rewards" can be provided with little or no financial investment. In the upcoming chapters, I'll share some ideas for how you can put these powerful tools to work for you!

CHAPTER TWO

Recognizing the Power Within

Before you can successfully capitalize on the resources of your employees, you must first understand *what really motivates people.*

Still think it's money?

Think about it for a moment. If it were really just about money, who would ever teach, risk their lives in law enforcement or hold an elected position? Fortunately, for all of us who have the responsibility of filling positions and motivating employees, there are many more compelling – and less expensive – factors. Recognition, a sense of contribution and a sense of belonging help create loyal employees who naturally deliver great customer service.

These motivators apply to employees in every type of business. For instance, a friend was recently raving about the software company where she works. She filled more than half of our lunch hour with story after story about her boss, the CEO, all the recognition she was receiving and her gratitude at finding such a great company. Much later she mentioned, almost as an aside, that her new employer didn't pay as well as some of her previous ones but *she didn't care!* What mattered to her were all the policies and practices that made her feel valued as an employee.

As a business owner, I can assure you the most important recognition **my** business received was being voted "Best Place to Work" in Washington State. After a few years in business, we participated in an annual survey conducted by a local business magazine, *Washington CEO*. The competition was judged through blind surveys of our staff in every area, from sales, to administration, to delivery. Because of the resounding praise of our employees, we became the first retailer to EVER earn such an honor. Each year we participated, we won or placed in our size category.

These same voices are the ones heard by our customers when they visit our stores. As a result, Sleep Country USA rapidly grew from a single store in January of 1991, to eight stores by the end of the first year. By the middle of 1999, there were 28 stores, and it's still growing! That type of growth is impossible to achieve alone. It requires a committed team with common goals and objectives.

Okay, we know it's hard enough to get your own

family to agree on how to budget family funds or which project to tackle next. So how do you get a group of unrelated people with no obvious investment to consistently act in the best interest of your company and customers?

Remember, this challenge is not unique to business owners. Anyone promoted to management finds him or herself going from being responsible for his or her own work to being responsible for the work of others. The measure of your contribution to the organization changes from that of your own productivity to the productivity of your team.

Catch 'em at their best

So how do you build a team dedicated to the company, customer and excellence? So many geographic areas are experiencing changing labor markets and the Pacific Northwest is no exception. During growth periods, the proliferation of jobs and allure of rapidly expanding high tech fields can make recruiting even more challenging. When labor markets ARE tight, employees can be pickier and discerning about the companies where they choose to work.

It's not enough to offer competitive salaries and comprehensive benefits. 401K plans and insurance packages are standard in today's competitive employment market. These items, formerly known as "benefits," are now just the price of admission and businesses are continually challenged to find more ways to attract and retain the indispensable competitive "secret weapon" known as *people*!

Think of your employees as internal customers. Determine the mindset of this particular group of "customers" the same way you evaluate your end consumers. This is actually easier than you think. The good news is, it doesn't require costly, complicated market studies, focus groups or consultants.

The number one employee motivator is **RECOGNITION** – the easiest, cheapest thing we can give our staff and the one thing we give least often. I've spent a lot of time thinking about why we give so little recognition. It's not because managers are evil ogres.

In business, I believe it's largely because we're conditioned to spend time solving problems. We act as "firefighters," running around with our imaginary extinguishers, from one "fire" to the next.

In fact, if we could shift our focus to catching people doing things RIGHT instead of WRONG, we would probably have far fewer "fires" to extinguish.

So how do you catch your staff doing things right? It's not always easy. It's not because "right" things aren't happening this very minute, but rather because we're not always there to see them.

We often oversee people who work in multiple

locations during various hours of operation. There is often no way to personally catch everyone in the act of doing things right. So what do you do?

At various companies where I've worked, we utilized a number of methods to catch our people doing things right. Retail businesses and restaurants often employ mystery shoppers or phantom diners to give them candid feedback. These services can provide some positive results. They not only give you an indication of areas which need improvement, but also allow you to catch people in the act of *doing things right.*

If you decide to use a mystery shopper type service, tell your staff so they don't feel spied on. We shared the logic behind using such services as a way to identify necessary improvements, as well as recognizing excellence. We also shared the actual "shopper" survey form so they knew what we expected. Then we designed and implemented a reward system to recognize great results.

The questionnaire has evolved over the years, as has the scoring. However, for many years, a five was perfect. You no doubt have already gathered I don't believe in using money as the prime employee motivator. Nonetheless, this is one instance where we did use money – five bucks to be exact. It wasn't about the amount, but how the money was awarded.

"Five Bucks for a Perfect Five" is how we billed

the shopping report recognition program. Once we compiled the monthly shopping reports, we would count the number of perfect "fives" and I would head to the bank for crisp, five-dollar bills.

Do you have a monthly meeting where everyone attends? If so, this is the ideal setting to show off your new role as Company Cheerleader! At our mandatory monthly sales meetings, the sales manager read the list of "perfect fives." I ran around the room handing out five-dollar bills and high fives to those who earned them.

We did not mention those who earned fours or any score lower than five. No one was belittled or singled out for low scores. Instead, we simply recognized those with perfect fives. Having colleagues around you receive recognition and knowing you fell short of obviously attainable goals is a powerful motivator for improving performance.

Our number of winners grew over time. After a while, even our local bank tellers knew something great was going on at Sleep Country USA. Each month, we'd request a growing stack of crisp, five-dollar bills. I always looked through them carefully at the counter and ask for replacements for worn bills.

When they asked –and they would ask – I was happy to explain that we handed the bills out at sales meetings to recognize employees who received perfect scores from our mystery shopper service.

Not a bad little bit of marketing, actually. Wouldn't you prefer to shop at a store that utilized self-evaluation techniques, especially one where you knew the sales force scored high in customer service?

Another technique we used for catching our people "doing things right" was with Thank You /Reply Cards. It was a strictly enforced policy that sales staffs send each Sleep Country customer a handwritten note thanking them for their valued business.

Yes, we counted. Our computers told us how many sales orders each salesperson generated monthly. They put their initials in the upper left corner of the envelope by the return address and sent the completed cards to the office via inner-office mail for outgoing postage. The receptionist kept tallies for each salesperson and issued weekly status reports via email detailing their card-to-order ratio to date.

No salesperson was eligible for Salesperson of the Month or allowed to earn awards in our monthly sales contests unless they achieved 100% on their Thank You Cards. *If you tell them it's important, be ready to keep track and tie something they care about to the results!*

Remember – as you saw with the practice of getting crisp, five-dollar bills from the local bank – your recognition tools can also serve as marketing opportunities. I must admit I firmly believe EVERYTHING you do in your business is marketing. This was certainly true for our handwritten thank you cards, as well.

Surveys show we currently receive so few handwritten thank you cards that when we do, we tell an average of seven people! That's a lot of marketing for the price of a postage stamp!

Our "Thank You Card" provided an area for the sales associate to write the customer a personal note thanking them for their business and assuring them their purchase was a good investment. The other portion of the card was a detachable, postage paid reply card for the customer to use in evaluating their shopping experience.

The card asked the customer to rate their shopping experience on a scale of 1 to 5, using a variety of criteria. These ranged from store appearance to sales associate knowledge, competitive pricing to delivery. Then it asked the critical question, "Would you recommend Sleep Country USA to a friend?" Lastly, we provided an open section inviting the customer's freelance remarks.

I know from experience with other business people that some of you cringe at the thought of putting a postage-paid reply card in the hands of each and every one of your customers. Too many businesses believe "no news is good news," but the reality is, with all the choices available to today's consumers, no business can afford to ignore its performance and shortcomings.

So relax, we did this for **YEARS,** with literally tens of thousands of customers annually. I agree it's more human nature to complain than praise. However, even with this easy-to-use, no-cost method of communication, our complaints barely measured a fraction of a percent.

Once, a customer complained about our comment card. He didn't like the idea of "giving people an easy way to rag on some poor employee just trying to do a job." He obviously believed we intended to catch people doing things *wrong.* I contacted him and explained the information was not used to the detriment of the sales or delivery staffs, but instead allowed customers to help us catch staff doing things *right.* I also shared our complaint statistics with him, and he quickly became a supporter of our program, even putting the practice to work in his own organization!

While traveling with my husband, a writer, on a promotional tour for his book, we stayed in more than our share of hotels. One major hotel chain provided a survey card at every turn. They were on the front desk as we checked in, on tables in the lobby, restaurant and bar, and even in our room. The hotel made its intent obvious through the card's bold heading, "Catch Me at My Best."

Designing a comment card for your business is

easy. ***Don't start from scratch.*** When you are out
and about in stores and restaurants, pick up a copy
of their comment cards. Once you've collected several examples, study the elements of each that
appeal to you. Just remember to keep it *short, simple and easy to use.*

Pass your paste-up sample around the office to
get feedback from your team, or run it by as many
typical consumers as you can before you put it into
production. Family and friends make great "typical
consumers" because they often point out where we
use too much industry jargon or made things too
complicated. A sample of the comment card I
designed for Sleep Country USA is included at the
back of this book.

The single most critical element is to insure you
can identify your customer through your cards. We
did not rely on the customer to fill in their name and
address. We believed it was so critical to contact
unhappy customers and address problems that our
sales associates filled in the computer-generated
sales order number on the reply portion of the card
prior to mailing it. With this computer identification
number we could contact customers, as well as identify the appropriate salesperson or delivery team for
applicable training or recognition.

Your sales staff must not be afraid of this important communication tool! During the initial training

each associate receives, we addressed not only the value of repairing damaged customer relationships, but also the positive benefits stemming from these cards.

None of us likes to deal with complaints or unhappy customers. But given the significant advertising investment spent to bring that customer through the door, the time the sales associate devoted to serving them and the expense incurred in delivering the product to their home, isn't it worth a little extra time and effort to insure their satisfaction? Remember how many people YOU told about the last negative experience you had with a business? Can you really afford to ignore even ONE complaint?

In a few special situations where we knew, despite our best efforts to make things right, that bad feelings lingered, we sent flowers to the customer's office with a brief note of apology. Think about it for a minute. What happened the last time flowers arrived at your office? Didn't everyone who walked by admire them and inquire, "Who sent the flowers?"

Sending flowers to an unhappy customer forces them to say, "You know that bad experience I told you I had at that store last weekend? The flowers are from them." Don't worry about opening a string of "What happened?" questions. Trust me, *they already know*. Your customer already gave them the story in full detail! The flowers not only soothe the sting, but also neutralize "bad press."

Rest assured, with a postage-paid reply card in the hands of every one of your customers, you will receive SOME complaints. But this is a valuable snapshot of your business, and while a single card may describe an isolated incident, more than one comment regarding the same associate, store or policy is a sure indication an issue needs immediate attention.

If you utilize mystery shoppers, you can send them in to get more specific information about a problem the cards illustrated. In our ten-year history, we only had one situation where this was necessary. The comment cards were the first indication of a problem at a store in the chain. The mystery shopping service helped us identify the problem's root so it could be solved promptly. By working with the store manager, we were able to rearrange personnel to eliminate the internal conflicts customers described as creating an "uncomfortable environment for shopping."

You will also get some amusing mail. I've even laminated a handful over the years to use as part our training to help overcome salespeople's fears of such cards.

One I particularly liked rated us the highest in every category, but when answering "Would you recommend Sleep Country USA to a friend?" checked "NO." At first I was concerned about what could have possibly gone wrong, until I read the handwritten remark. It read, "I have no friends." These were always good for a laugh, not only when I speak to business groups, but within our company as well. Don't hesitate to share these gems with your staff. It really is okay to have fun at work!

Most likely what you'll find is an abundance of mail extolling the virtues of your staff. Customers repeatedly tell of salespeople who worked with their families long after the posted closing time, but never pressured them to buy. First time customers are often thrilled with the education they received, helping them make an informed decision.

Reading customer reply cards was one of the most uplifting things I did each day. It was a nice balance reading about all the GREAT service customers experience in our stores on a regular basis. Wouldn't you like some good news today?

Spread the love

You already know how important it is to promptly handle complaints, but what do you do with all the kudos? Praise, like discipline, needs to be timely. But unlike discipline, praise also needs to be VERY public.

Remember, this praise doesn't belong to you; it

belongs to the person who earned it. At one of my speeches, a woman approached me afterwards to tell me how great she thought it was that we share the positive comments we receive about our staff. She worked for a large department store that filled a lot of special orders for customers. They had cards at the counter to give customers and include with items they sent to them, and she did so regularly.

Although she gave out countless cards, she never saw a single one returned. She rightly refused to believe out of all those customers, not a single one bothered to fill out the simple, postage-paid card to recognize her efforts. More likely, the cards were filling up her personnel file in some manager's office, rather than encouraging her to go the extra mile for the next customer.

It is also possible to design a feedback card for your vendors, in order to catch your office staff doing things right. This card may ask things like: Are orders clear and accurate? Are calls returned in a timely manner? Vendors are important partners in your business and those relationships can help insure your success. You can mail cards to a few letters of the alphabet each month to keep a steady flow of comments coming in.

The feedback may identify areas needing attention or processes requiring streamlining. Making those changes will likely improve morale, as they'll make everyone's jobs easier. Be sure to allow a place for the vendor to make remarks regarding specific employees who make their job easier or more pleasant. That way, you'll have even more praise to pass around.

This recognition has little value to the employee – or to the next customer who walks through your door – if it's locked away in a personnel file. The many great comment cards you receive should be passed to those deserving praise in front of peers. Your monthly sales, office or group meetings are great venues for sharing this "good news."

Don't hesitate to read a few exceptional ones out loud. You'll be sharing your idea of great customer service through real life examples that establish your service standard. You'll also prove what can be done, and in doing so, inspire others to do the same.

Depending on the relationship you have with your staff and the lavish praise of the customer, you may be able to have some fun with this. Sometimes I would follow the most gushing comments by adding, "love, Mom." Remember, having fun at work is a good thing, but if you haven't yet created a light-hearted environment with your team, wait until you are sure this sort of antic will get a laugh and not detract from well-deserved praise.

The most important thing is to publicly state, through your actions, that you value extra efforts.

Do not underestimate the power and addiction of employee recognition! The more you give, the harder they'll work to earn more! Once you establish a culture of excellence and praise, you'll uncover fewer problems to address and a more receptive audience for discussing needed improvements.

The purpose of recognition is to build a high performance team that naturally delivers excellent customer service and frightens competitors from your door. Sometimes, that's accomplished through awards and other signs of appreciation. Other times, it's subtler and simply about creating an environment where doing a good job comes naturally.

The new phrase I've heard bantered about is "working outside your job description." I've historically been that kind of employee. Looking back, it's partially true this was a result of my own personality and upbringing, but it was also nurtured by working in environments where I knew my extra efforts were welcomed and recognized.

Perception becomes reality

If you want to change results, change the perception. Employees deliver service equal to how they perceive themselves and their role in the organization. A case in point: Sleep Country delivery crews carried tools to assemble daybeds, attach headboards to new bed frames and so forth. However, instead of equipping drivers with toolboxes, we gave them sturdy briefcases, the kind portrayed in ads as virtually indestructible, even when an elephant stood on them. We also gave them business cards.

Why briefcases and business cards? Who carries these accessories? *Professionals.*

How would you prefer your delivery people view themselves, as manual laborers or delivery professionals? The briefcases and business cards served as subtle forms of recognition. They said we valued their roles in the company and saw them as equal members of a team whose job it was to "wow" customers.

Sure, they gave their business cards to family and friends, but each time they did, their shoulders were square and they showed pride in their jobs and the company.

In addition to improved attitude and job performance, this pride manifested itself in other surprising ways. Our company holiday party was held in a hotel ballroom. One year, a woman in the hallway outside the party stopped an assistant on the delivery team. She asked if he worked for Sleep Country. When he said yes, she asked what he did for the company. He looked her in the eye and replied, "Ma'am, I'm one of Sunny's goodwill ambassadors. How may I help you?"

She explained her company was playing a game – word had leaked that I was in the building and a prize was offered for my autograph. (Trust me; appear in your own television and radio ads for nearly a decade and this sort of thing will happen to you too!) He told her he'd see what he could do and went off to find me.

He found me, explained the game and added, "You know, we could sell a whole lot of mattresses if we just walked across the hall for five minutes." That's exactly what we did; we paid a visit to the other party, shook hands, signed autographs and then rejoined our event. He was right about that simple act. I saw it mentioned on comment cards for over a year, as several partygoers came to our company to purchase mattresses.

When employees have pride in their work, it shows and customers respond favorably. For example, a fabulous supper club, The Velvet Room in Scottsdale, Arizona, gives its wait staff business cards. Not just cards from the club to carry, but their own *personal* cards. After a delightful evening, largely the result of our waiter's personal, yet professional, service, we asked him to repeat his name. He not only told us, but also gave us one of his cards so we could ask for him again when we made future reservations.

The wait staff influences much of a dining experience. The best in this profession build repeat customers who ask for them by name. Customers like to return to places where they are known and recognized, where waiters may even remember their favorite beverage. What a simple way to encourage this sort of relationship between staff and diners. How many new customers does each member of the wait staff attract as they go about their daily lives, circulating their business cards and inviting people to "ask for me when you come in, I'd love to take care of you."

In the long run, *every form* of recognition pays back far more than it costs. It may not always be something you can track and measure, but your customers *feel it* nonetheless. Using these simple tools, you begin to build a high performance team for whom delivering excellent customer service is natural and seemingly effortless. This team, loyal to your company and dedicated to your customers, will take you to new heights and leave even your competitors in awe of your success.

CHAPTER THREE

Your Very Own Fun and Games Department

So now that you've traded in your fire extinguisher for cheerleading pom-poms, it's time to really start having fun! As one of my first bosses, an accidental motivational genius used to say, "If we're not having fun, we're doing something wrong."

Not only is it "okay" to have fun at work, statistics show it's actually beneficial. Most likely you've seen some of the same surveys I have in recent years documenting what I know is true. Healthy, fun work environments improve productivity while reducing absenteeism, as well as employee turnover. Now, I'm not proposing you turn your workplace into a sandbox, but there are countless ways to improve results while having fun. I like to call it your very own "Fun and Games Department."

A Fun and Games Department doesn't need a big budget or a special office. In fact, since you are the

only full time member of the "department" it operates wherever you are and utilizes whatever
resources you have at your disposal.

One very successful bank chain provides each
branch manager with a kit for both employee recognition and community involvement. It included samples of various programs used successfully in other
branches as well as sourcing information.

Don't worry if no one gave you such a kit. You
already have everything you need right at your fin-
gertips. A great place to start is with that super tool
on your desktop – the computer in front of you. You
can generate great award certificates, whimsical
recognition posters and even greeting cards – all for
the price of paper and ink!

There's no rule requiring everything to be store
bought, no rule that says only an engraved plaque
counts. And if your staff hasn't received any form of
recognition on a consistent basis, they won't be picky!

If you're not the "creative type," tap those on
your team who are to come up with fun and interesting ways to reward and inspire your employees.
Ask other business people what successful tactics
they utilize for employee recognition. Borrow from
as many sources as you can! I've collected ideas
from every place I've ever worked, adapting them to
new situations or just putting my own spin on them.

There's a popular misconception that employee

incentives and rewards are the company's responsibility. I've met many managers, particularly those in middle management, who say, "Our Company doesn't do those sort of things." To which I reply, "Then why don't YOU?" So for managers, team leaders, even office personnel who feel they need specific appointments to do jobs that clearly need doing, allow me the honor.

"I hereby appoint YOU head of your company's Fun and Games Department."

That has been my internal title at almost every company I've worked for, regardless of my official position. I've taken it so far as to sign related emails and memos "Your Very Own Fun & Games Department." It doesn't take people long to figure out what's going on and it certainly sets the tone!

Recognition is a great problem-solving tool. When we first added e-mail to our company computer system, the biggest challenge was getting everyone to check it on a regular basis. Employees would quickly read mail from me or other managers, but their colleagues complained their messages were largely ignored.

Rather than allow everyone to get off on the wrong foot, considering this new tool a hassle or source of grief, I went out and bought a handful of $10 gift certificates to some popular lunch spots. I distributed a couple to each office staffer, instructing them to select certain of their group e-mails to the stores and make a note at the bottom – "The first one to read this just earned a $10 lunch certificate." From the history the computer provided, it was easy to see who read the mail when, and declare a clear winner.

By passing gift certificates out to everyone in the office, employees at the different stores quickly caught on to the benefits of reading e-mail, regardless of who sent it. Word spread quickly and employees rushed madly to read e-mail. Since not every office staffer used their certificates right away, employees remained unsure which e-mails would offer lunch, so they read all of them. After a month, the certificates were distributed and store personnel were in the habit of checking e-mail.

Rising above challenges

In addition to budget constraints, sometimes our physical office layouts also present challenges to giving recognition. When I worked as a secretary in a large telemarketing sales department, staffers spent their days sequestered in cubicles. All day they made calls, took orders, solved problems and had very little interaction with each other. The company was a large, international conglomerate. Every month I prepared sales reports tracking individual results and submitted them to anonymous offices much higher up the food chain.

Recognizing the environment was demoralizing to good salespeople, the supervisor of the telemarketing department took it upon himself to change what he could. Company policy wouldn't allow him to remove the cubicle workstations and frankly, they were needed to block sound. Nonetheless, it was important to foster interaction and tap into the natural competitiveness of the sales professionals.

One afternoon, as I prepared to leave after spending the entire day compiling monthly sales reports, the supervisor stopped me. He asked if I had anything pressing to do that evening or could I stay to help with a project? He then asked where we could get some helium filled balloons nearby. I directed him to a local party and crafts store. Once there, he selected eight different colored balloons and asked the clerk to leave the ribbon tails on the balloons very, very long.

We struggled to get the lively balloons crammed into the backseat of his car for the short drive back to the office. On the way, he explained my role in the new project. He wanted me to use my big, permanent markers to decorate each of the balloons for the top salesperson in each of the eight product and performance categories the company tracked.

At my desk, with the balloons and my box of magic markers, it was easy to label them with phrases like "Salesperson of the Month" and "Top XYZ

Product Sales." I added some squiggles, made them look colorful and festive, but now what? As I finished, the supervisor emerged again from his office and said, "Oh wow, those look great. Grab your report, let's go."

With the Monthly Sales report in hand, we took the appropriate decorated balloon to the cubicles of the peak performers. The purpose of the extra long ribbon tails quickly became apparent, as he tied the balloon to the adjustment knob of each person's chair. Those long, colorful ribbons let the balloon float high above the confining cubicle walls. As we left for the day, I looked back at our handiwork from the doorway. It was a sight to behold. Eight colorful, decorated, helium balloons bounced at the end of long, bright ribbons. It was like a room full of smiles.

I anxiously awaited the arrival of the sales staff the next morning. From my desk, I could see the looks on their faces as they came through the door. One by one, and in small groups, they appeared in the doorway. Each stopped abruptly with similar startled expressions. It was like they had just walked into a surprise party.

Then the realization of the purpose of the balloons hit them and they *dashed* to their cubicles "Oh my gosh, that's my desk!" Suddenly they were giving each other high-fives over the walls of their workstations, and coming around to congratulate each other.

A little later, I saw the friendly competitiveness of true sales professionals surface, with banter like "Hey, this order I just wrote is going to really let the air out of your balloon this month!," followed by replies like, "Well, we'll see whose chair it's tied to again next month. I think it looks great right where it is!"

As the secretary who eventually cut the snarl of ribbons from the wheels of the chairs, I can tell you **NO ONE** ever took the balloon off their own chair. They'd come in the next day and lament over the absence of their dead balloon. I'd just smile and say, "I guess you'll have to earn another one."

Each person on that team of telemarketing sales professionals later moved on to outside sales and had long, productive careers with the company. Many moved into management. The supervisor was also promoted based on the impressive performance of his group. Even I moved up to a bigger office to be the "fun and games department" for a whole new group of salespeople.

I learned a valuable lesson from those balloons. I saw how people came alive when praised, even in a simple way. When that supervisor pulled out his wallet every month to pay for those balloons, he made a small out-of-pocket expenditure, but a huge personal investment.

Taking praise public

This is just one more idea to get your creative juices flowing. There are countless other ways to give your employees well-deserved recognition. If your company has a newsletter, use this venue to share things you have caught people "doing right." Everyone loves to see his or her name or picture in print. If they are featured, give them a few extra copies to pass on to family and friends.

What about your company website? The Internet has become the equivalent of the world's "refrigerator door." People post all sorts of things, some personal, some business, some informative, others just for fun.

Sleep Country has a site page dedicated to "Employees," featuring award winners for the month in sales, delivery, office and warehousing. If you can include a photo of the honored employee, that's even better.

Delivery team members told me they direct their families, particularly those who live out-of-state, to the company website whenever their names are listed as award recipient. We don't bring report cards home to our parents anymore, but having our name in the company newsletter or on the website is one way we can share our accomplishments and pride in a job well done.

If the newsletter or website are not in your area

of responsibility, have lunch with the person whose job it is and inspire them to join your "Fun & Games Department." One of the best things about this "department" is you can recruit anyone to join!

As you're looking for ways to recognize your employees, consider utilizing current resources in different ways. An example: parking became an issue when we expanded our offices. Spots near the door were coveted, especially during the rainy winter months. So we took three of the best spots and ordered signs designating them for "Employee of the Month," "Driver of the Month" and "Assistant Driver of the Month". Every day of the month, those individuals received a very welcome form of recognition.

Basic office supplies easily double as recognition tools and should be fixtures of your "Fun & Games Department." Bright highlighting magic markers, colorful stickers and attention getting paper all work wonders.

A generic bulletin board can become the center of attention when you add a banner (generated on your computer if need be) that reads, "The Good News Board."

We've had such a board in most of the companies where I've worked. It's essential to have a regular place or time when recognition is handed out. Please don't wait until the year-end party! Make

"Good News" part of your every day!

It's important to explain your Good News Board to your staff as a group. Tell them, "This is our new Good News Board. You are welcome to put anything on this board that represents good news. If you just had a new grandchild, put up a photo. Your child got straight A's on their report card, post a copy here. We will be happy to share any and all good news with you."

Be sure to remind them "this board is NOT for any state required posters. No snippy notes about keeping the lunchroom clean. There are other places for that sort of communication, this is strictly for good news."

Don't be afraid to put this board in a prominent place in your office. I'm not sure why it is that businesses so often hide great news about their company. Restaurants certainly don't! Have you ever been to a restaurant that DIDN'T post positive reviews on the wall for everyone to see? Next time you are waiting for a table, take a look at the date on those reviews! Some of them are years old, yet they hang there still, subtly encouraging you to wait those 45 minutes for a table, quietly assuring you the experience is worth the wait.

Often business people tell me they don't need internal sales tactics. They tell me no one ever comes into their building because they are in an industrial complex or some such thing. I always inquire further whenever I hear this. "You mean the mail isn't delivered every day?"

"Oh sure," they reply.

"What about package deliveries? Couriers and the like?" I query.

"Oh, we get lots of those."

"People get lost and come in for directions? Need help finding other businesses in the area? Use the telephone book?"

"Yes, all the time. It's so easy to get turned around in these office parks."

"What about your staff? Do they have a special entrance or do they typically use the front door?"

By now they usually catch on. You might not think the people who deliver your mail and packages or get lost in your building are your customers, but they may KNOW one of your future or present customers. If they are waiting for the receptionist to sign their form or hand them a directory, and they see all this "Good News" about your company, it may spark interest about your business. Not only could they refer customers to you – they could refer future employees – or even apply for jobs themselves!

Don't underestimate the value of displaying items for your current staff either. What better way to tell you are proud of their accomplishments than to announce them where all can see? What better way to remind them on a daily basis about all the "Good News" in and about your company, to inspire their loyalty and build pride in where they work?

Sometimes we're so busy focusing on our external customers in the marketplace we overlook our essential internal customers – our employees!

If you are new to the role of "cheerleader," a Good News Board is a simple way to start. One good thing about a big, blank bulletin board staring you in the face – it forces you to find "Good News" to post on it.

We posted cards and letters from customers regarding outstanding service regularly. While we distributed the sales letters to applicable stores (handed out at our monthly sales meeting, of course), we posted office and delivery related ones in our office/distribution center.

When we got raves from customers via mail, fax or email, I added my own "Great Job" comments in my signature purple highlighter, plus an accolade sticker. We also posted these on the "Good News Board."

If you think people in your office won't get jazzed about a posted note with comments and a sticker, rest assured I once thought the same. Surely, professional delivery drivers wouldn't care about such a juvenile thing. I was wrong!

Once, a great letter regarding a couple delivery team members came while I was out of town. My assistant, realizing praise – like discipline – is best when handed out promptly, left a copy of the letter in my in box and posted the original on the "Good News Board."

When I returned, I saw the posted letter before reading the one in my desk tray. I immediately recognized it as one I hadn't seen before, since it lacked my signature squiggles and sticker. Pausing to read it, I was most impressed. The customer raved about the delivery team's courtesy and professionalism, extra efforts and great humor. I thought, "Wow! They did a great job!" Then I noticed the handwritten note in the lower right corner. It read, "Where's my sticker?"

I immediately went to my desk and sorted through my sticker collection for the biggest one. I stuck it over the question and added my own, "There." The next day I found a simple reply: "Thank you!"

There is NO ONE in your organization who won't benefit from a little recognition. Start building your very own fun and games department today! With it you will build a high performance, problem solving, customer satisfaction machine your competitors will fear!

CHAPTER FOUR

Sales Contest Magic

Walk into just about any company with a sales force and you will see plaques or trophies for Salesperson of the Month. These awards usually go to the top volume writer in the company, and quite often the honor regularly passes back and forth between two or three top performers.

At Sleep Country, a retail chain with stores of various sizes and different volume potentials, we wanted a more equitable way to decide this important award. In reality, it's just as hard for a person in a smaller store to reach 110% of their quota, as it is for a person in a large volume store. So we considered the accomplishment equal, though there may have been a significant disparity between the actual dollar amounts sold.

We awarded "points" for every percentage point over the individual volume goal (i.e. 110% = 10 points). Since we always wanted to insure profitability, each salesperson had a profit dollar goal, as well as a volume goal. The same scoring applied to this part of the equation. (104% = 4 points for a total of 14 points.) The top "point earner" was our Salesperson of the Month. In the event of a tie, actual profit dollars broke the tie, because it's not enough to write a lot of business, it should be profitable business as well!

Using this method, we drew our Salesperson of the Month from every store in the chain, regardless of size. Sometimes they were the overall "top writer," but often they were not. Because this system worked off an "over goal" percentage, everyone had a chance to win. It motivated the sales staff because they knew the playing field was level, and it put the coveted award within everyone's grasp.

If you've ever run track, this is similar to what's known as your Personal Record or "PR." While runners who **place** in races are always recognized, so are all runners whose performances break their "PRs". It **is** considered as big a deal to break your personal performance record, as it is to come in first. This is the same sort of environment you want to create for your sales team to keep them all running hard and striving for their best, even if they can't always come in first.

Common mistakes

Most companies who rely on sales professionals long ago embraced the motivating magic of sales contests, or at least believe the have. In the standard world of sales contests, companies often typically make a couple of major mistakes resulting in countless missed opportunities.

They keep going, and going . . .

The first common mistake is for sales contests to run too long. It's hard to keep everyone's "eyes on the prize" for much longer than three months. If you're forced to work within a rigid company sales contest structure, you'll have to find ways to keep the spark alive for the entire contest period.

We had a situation like this at the international conglomerate where I first gained much of my business experience. Each year the company provided an all-expenses paid trip for the **every** qualifying salesperson and his or her spouse to a resort destination. They called it the Sales Achievement Club. After earning this award, salespeople were recognized as "club members" with plaques, special designations on their business cards, pins and more. Every sales person who hit his or her quota for the year was eligible for club membership.

Company headquarters annually assigned quotas based on territory values, past performance and expected growth. Sales people received their quotas at the beginning of the year. Every month, a few weeks after the monthly numbers were tallied; they released updates to keep everyone posted on how they were doing.

The excitement of checking your name on the long list of regional participants quickly faded. The motivational genius I mentioned earlier felt there must be some way to keep the prize more visible and the team motivated. He wanted to be sure they were **all** on the trip, although it wasn't awarded until 15 months AFTER the date it was first announced. (Three months after the close of the sales year, no doubt allowing time for order cancellations to impact results.)

I've already admitted to historically working "outside my job description" and this was one of those times. With this challenge before me, I tapped into my creativity. Armed with only poster board and general office supplies, I went to work.

Using a map, I divided the distance between where we were (Dallas, Texas) and where they were going for Club that year (Maui, Hawaii) into twelve mostly equal parts. I found a town, landmark or body of water to represent how far along they should be in their "journey" each month.

Then I made a colorful wall chart on poster board. I listed the sales staff names down the left side and the target towns or landmarks across the top. I also wrote comments under the monthly "stops." For the month where they should have been as far as the desert it said: "Sand but no ocean, better keep going!" The last two months were in the Pacific Ocean with warnings about sharks or hoping they could swim. Remember, the object is not just to succeed, but also to have fun doing it!

Each month, when the results arrived in the mail, I took my wide-tipped magic marker and extended the line from each salesperson's name to the place they landed on our map. Sometimes they made it to May, and it was only April. Other times they were only as far as September, in November. Either way, this chart, posted in the center of our office (right beside the coffee pot), served as a colorful, daily reminder of what was needed to achieve their goals.

Monthly sales standings reviews, once a few minutes perusing a typed and stapled list, became standing room only events. The entire team gathered as I colored in the bars beside their names. Cheers and friendly jeers could be heard in the offices down the hall as we posted the results each month.

This simple illustration kept the prize visible for the entire year and tapped into the natural competitiveness of the sales professionals. Because they could all attend if they hit their goals, they encouraged friends who lagged behind by teasing that they would send them a postcard if they didn't make it. It became virtually impossible to give up with that many eyes watching their progress.

As previously explained, there are ways to work within any contest structure to insure maximum participation and results. Personally, I favor monthly contests. That way, if some staffers do get discouraged because they aren't going to win *this month*, it's not too long before a new month begins and they can get fired up again.

Bigger doesn't always mean better

The second most common mistake is to offer too big a prize. In justifying the expense to the company for such extravagance, contests are often not only too long, but too complicated. With only one prize and too many rules to qualify, salespeople might decide superhuman performance is required to win. Not only is the average salesperson unlikely to try, they may actually resent what they view as "jumping through hoops."

What's wrong with one big, really awesome prize? Depending on how it's handled, maybe nothing. But consider for a moment the thought processes of salespeople in your organization. At the sales meeting when you announce the new sales contest and award, instantly the bottom half of your sales staff tunes out when they realize there's only one prize. They know there is no way for them to win, because they are not consistent top performers. And frankly, this is probably the group most needing motivation, because it is already not exceeding performance goals.

Every company has well-known top salespeople who consistently outperform other team members. All the sales people know who the "stars" are. When the average or slightly above average performers on your team hear there is only one award, they might say to themselves "Well, you know so and so is going to win. They always do."

If you are really unlucky, they might say it out loud! In either event, rest assured it's what *more than half* of them are thinking. As the contest progresses and it becomes clear who the front-runners are, another quarter of the team starts to lose interest because they can't catch the leader. By the last week of the contest, you have only a couple real contenders who are expending every effort to win the prize. Odds are, they're the same peak performers who would deliver with or without the prize.

Can you achieve your company's sales goals with just a handful of players? If so, do you even need the rest of them? Chances are, your company would be more successful if *every team member* tried to do just a little bit better, rather than relying on the superhuman efforts of one or two.

That's why I prefer lots of smaller prizes, lots of winners and an easy-to-follow set of contest guidelines. At Sleep Country USA, we built our company by offering *every single salesperson an opportunity to win a prize every single month of the year!* To win, all they had to do was hit their personal sales goals and send 100% of their thank you cards to customers.

Before the budget watchers have a stroke, let me say these are NOT big prizes. Usually they are something like a dinner gift certificate. If you are still adding up the number of salespeople on your team and doing the math on all those gift certificates, let me remind you that sales contests shouldn't actually cost the company *anything*.

If you don't have goals allowing you to give any salesperson that hits them a dinner gift certificate, the solution is simple – raise the goals! You shouldn't have to make them unattainable to cover the nominal cost of such an item. In fact, I doubt the increase would be noticeable to most sales professionals. They would probably be so delighted to have a carrot; they might not care if it was an inch further away.

We called these "Level One" prizes and everyone could win. There were also other prizes for higher levels of achievement and often a "grand prize" a step above the others. But the secret to successful sales contests is to have more winners more often, because more of your team will play.

In fact, there were months when 80% of our

sales staff walked out of sales meetings with *something* for their efforts. Is it any wonder our stores set industry records for sales and profits? What could your company do if 80% of *your* sales force hit their goals each month? Now you know why I call it the magic of sales contests!

Cash prizes

But why a prize or dinner gift certificate? Why not just give them cash? Wouldn't most people prefer cold, hard cash? Perhaps, but would you be getting your money's worth? This is another common sales contest mistake.

What happened the last time *you* got a few extra bucks? Did they disappear into your wallet to be spent without a thought? Did you bet it on a football game? Did you apply it to a monthly bill? Have a shopping spree at lunch? Could you even tell me a week later how it was spent? Did your spouse even know you got it?

In retail establishments, salespeople are often asked to work hours that challenge their families. They work until nine on weeknights, so they usually aren't home to help with schoolwork or tuck in the little ones. Then they work weekends, because that's when consumers prefer to shop. The same is true with most major holidays. We knew families paid a price for the career our salespeople chose, so we tried to reward spouses as well. We recognized the sacrifices made by those at home and wanted to let them know we valued their families. But we also wanted to show them the contributions made at work were important.

Even if your sales force doesn't work the retail schedule, chances are those who excel put in extra hours, either in the office or at home. Your single salespeople also face the challenge of maintaining social lives. They often neglect family and friends while devoting time and energy to their careers.

We wanted to add to the quality of their lives at the same time we said thank you for a job well done. Many working families don't eat out often. A break from cooking usually means fast food, pizza or Chinese take-out. Couples with children often don't make time for "dates." If the salesperson is single, there's likely a friend or family member in their lives with whom a visit is long overdue.

Whereas cash quickly disappears into the black hole and is forgotten, the same is not true for a dinner gift certificate. A gift certificate covering an average dinner for two virtually requires you to *share it*.

Now the spouse comes home and announces, "Honey, we're going to try that new restaurant you've been talking about!" Other times, they load the whole family into the car and with your gift certificate, plus what they would normally spend on hamburgers, they get to share the world of cloth napkins and multiple forks with their children. They may get a neighbor to watch the kids for a few hours and rekindle the spark of their personal relationship. Maybe they just call a friend or sibling for that long overdue dinner.

Any way they use it, this small amount of money just became an event. They'll cherish the enhancement to their quality of life much longer than they'll remember a few bucks of extra spending money in their pocket.

Winning the home team

Including family and friends in the recognition is important because they have contributed to the success through their sacrifices. They need to know they're appreciated. When they don't feel the contribution is valued, family and friends are likely to encourage us to change jobs. "They don't appreciate all the hours you put in, why don't you go somewhere else?" a spouse or friend might ask.

Over the years, I heard from countless spouses that this is the best company their husband/wife has ever worked for. During a recent crisis, everyone was pushed to the limit. One of our veterans told me this story about coming home to his wife at the end of a particularly challenging day.

He closed his complaints about the day saying,

"I don't think I can do this anymore. It may be time to look for a new job."

His wife didn't miss a beat. "Honey, I know you've had a rough day and I'm sorry for that. But keep in mind this company has been very good to you, very good to *us*. We've been out to dinner, the theater, on weekend getaways, all sorts of things we wouldn't have done if you worked somewhere else. It wouldn't be right to bail now that they need you."

He told me that story after the crisis passed, when he was at yet another monthly sales meeting collecting his prize. So don't overlook the benefits of having the home team on your side

You know the rules, now break 'em.

Of course, the best thing about rules is breaking them from time to time. We occasionally had a single prize, such as an all-expense-paid trip to Bermuda. To insure full participation and keep everyone trying up to the very end, we awarded raffle tickets. You could earn five raffle tickets for what would typically be a Level One prize. You could earn more tickets, depending on how well you did. Sometimes there were bonus tickets for selling special products or Salesperson of the Month. Using the lotto mentality of "it only takes one ticket to win," everyone felt they at least had a shot.

Because the drawing took place only a couple of

weeks before the trip dates, most of the sales staff made arrangements for childcare or pet sitting since they were sure their ticket would be drawn. Those who didn't have a passport applied for one, "just in case." Company emails flew with the latest Internet weather report from Bermuda.

The day of the sales meeting when we drew for the trip, the raffle-spinning drum sat in plain view throughout the meeting. During the "business" of the meeting, we would stop to hand out raffle tickets to a few more salespeople. They would tear the stubs off and toss them in the drum. Finally, at the end of the meeting, all the tickets were in and it was time to draw. 'Round and 'round the drum spun until, with eyes closed, I reached in and drew the one magic ticket.

Everyone held his or her breath, waiting for me to call out the number. Digit by digit, until someone realized they were the big winner! The person who won had a wonderful trip, brought back small gifts for everyone in his store and his wife sent me a token gift and nice note as well. Years later I ran into him in another city and he is still talking about this trip!

We didn't do it often, but about once a year, we'd have a single big prize and play our own version of "Sleep Country Lotto," always to an enthusiastic crowd.

Other times, usually twice a year, we would

actually give away cash. I know, I know — I said I don't like cash and if it's "just cash" that's true. But once in awhile, you can have a lot of fun with cold, hard cash. Typically we would do these contests in fall with a "Money Tree," and again in spring with Easter Eggs.

The "Money Tree" was a real branch cut off a tree in my yard. I chose one that had lots of small tributary branches and looked like a miniature bare tree when stuck in a bucket of rocks. Stores that cater to teachers sell packets of tissue paper "leaves" to decorate bulletin boards and classrooms. These work perfectly as money tree leaves.

The leaves were worth $5, $10, $20, $50 and $100. Each salesperson earned leaves by reaching Level One (two leaves) and bonus leaves for greater achievement or special products, much in the way they earned raffle tickets. There were no limits on the number of leaves a person could earn! Remember, well-designed sales contests pay for themselves, so there's no need to limit performance!

Now, don't write the amounts on the leaves! This is part recognition, part game. You can code the leaves with simple designs, stickers or rubber stamped images. Just a little tip I learned along the way: make several designs equal the same amount of cash. Example, "these three designs all are worth $20 each." That way, it's not obvious which ones are the "high dollar" leaves when they're picking, because there aren't 50 of one design and only five of another. My rule of thumb is however many $100 bills I had on the tree, I tried not to have more than five more of any other single design to make it harder to "decode" as they were raking in their leaves. Trust me, they will try!

The morning of the sales meeting they walked in to see the "tree" no longer barren, but covered with fall leaves hanging by Christmas ornament hooks from the branches. At the end of the meeting, Salesperson of the Month picked first, followed by the person who earned the most leaves and continuing in descending order until the tree was bare.

I made a "code" sheet that I kept secret until everyone picked their leaves and had their pile in front of them. Then they sorted by the design stamped on the leaves and I would "decode" for them. "If you have a black cat, a ghost or a jack-o-lantern don't be frightened, those are each worth $10." They then turned in those designs and receive $10 bills on the spot. I did the same for each of the denominations. Since you made the leaves and know how many bills are on your tree, you can easily have cash ready to hand out. .

Each person counted their cash and announced how much they "raked in." Now, keep in mind that by now the monthly sales contests were well known at home, so the cash they earned, or most of it at least, was shared with those who contributed to their success.

The same principle applied to Easter Eggs, only instead of paper leaves and a decoder sheet, we used brightly colored plastic eggs that break in half. We folded each bill and stuffed it in the egg; snapped it shut and tossed it in a big basket. (No, you can't see the amount through the "shell." And yes, they tried.)

Salespeople then collected the number of eggs they earned in our annual Sleep Country USA Easter Egg Extravaganza. Even if you use cash, make sales contests fun and memorable to insure you get your money's worth, both in performance and positive attitudes!

More fun with sales contests

Other sales contests varied, with some based on seasonal or holiday themes. For example, January's contest results were announced the first week of February, so the January contest related to Valentine's Day. Level One earned staff money in accounts with a local florist for Valentine flowers. Top winners enjoyed "romance packages" at hotels with such luxuries as champagne and chocolates upon arrival, dinner for two, "rose petal turn-down service" and room service breakfast.

The "Garage Sale" let me clear all the "give

away" stuff we accumulated in the corner of our office. Here, staff earned the right to "shop" at the Sleep Country USA Garage Sale. For example, they selected from such treasures as a radio station Frisbee or promotional coffee mug. The "real" prizes that accompanied those items, kept secret at selection time, were a beach getaway and a Starbucks Coffee gift set, to name just two. If you choose a theme, carry it through. For example, employees arrived at the sales meeting that morning to find one of those hardware store orange and black plastic signs on the door reading, "GARAGE SALE Saturday Only 7:30am – 9:00am."

We also built a "game board" and played Sleep Country Jeopardy®. Modeled after the television game show, we used a tri-fold cardboard tabletop display, the kind kids use for school science fairs. We had dollar amount cards with questions on the back in various categories, such as PRODUCTS, HISTORY, CUSTOMER SERVICE, THE COM-PUTER even one called DO YOU DARE? Salespeople earned the right to answer questions of different dollar amounts from the category of their choice, and kept the cash when they answered correctly. With the exception of the oddities under "DO YOU DARE?" all questions were covered in our standard training and procedures.

This not only served as a fun way to give out

cash, but also as a training refresher for everyone. If someone didn't answer correctly, the "audience" shouted out the answer. It guaranteed they'd learn the answer to any question they missed – they were probably able to give the correct answer five years later! In true "game show" fashion, top winners also received the computer version of Jeopardy® (the real game) to play at home.

Other contests featured family tickets to the circus, dinner and theater tickets to Broadway touring shows, weekend getaways at nearby bed and breakfast inns – all sorts of things!

Our local zoo has an auction each year to raise money. It's one of my favorite charity events and can also provide innovative sales contests. One year they offered a scavenger hunt for 16 people, four teams of four each. The zoo docents provided food, beverages and the game. I offered prize money (easily divisible by four) and the zoo awarded blue ribbons, buttons and even a bucket of "zoo doo" for the last place team.

Using sales performance criteria, employees earned spots on the teams. At the zoo store, I bought four T-shirts in four different designs. We had a Wolf Team, Elephant Team, Gorilla Team and Lion Team. At the sales meeting where we announced the winners, each person received their team shirt and promptly pulled it on over their work clothes.

The zoo volunteers did a great job hosting the event. Teams consisted of salespeople from various stores, some of who never worked together before. Everyone had a great time and learned a lot about wildlife too. In addition, employees established long lasting camaraderie, and some team building took place.

Once a year, we offered a "Dress for Success" contest, in which employees earned gift certificates at business clothing stores. This contest gave winners well-deserved recognition, improved their career wardrobes and raised the overall professional appearance in our stores – all at the same time!

These are just a few ideas to get you thinking. Creative sales contests are great ways to motivate employees and award much-needed recognition. They build staff support for the company, and reinforce the employee's career choice with the folks at home. They can be used to reinforce training, improve professional appearance and add to your staff's quality of life. Oh yes, and they are *fun*. And, after all, you are your very own fun and games department!

CHAPTER FIVE

Making Meeting Magic

Another important element to consider is **when** to hand out recognition and awards. A logical time to give out sales awards is at your monthly sales meeting. If you don't already have one, you should.

Awards need to be timely. You may need a few days after the month "closes" to get the reports and results tallied, but sales meetings should then occur as soon as possible. Praise, like discipline, should be swift to be most effective.

If you already have a monthly meeting, use this chapter as a review to make sure you are maximizing the effectiveness of this important time. If you don't have a meeting but want to start one, here are some factors to consider as you plan.

Making your plan

Where should it be held? What time of day? What day of the week? Are the time and place optimum for all attendees? Often, companies plan meetings to best suit management schedules without realizing either the geography; day or time causes stress for attending staff. It's much easier to require management personnel to drive further, fight the traffic or leave their houses earlier than to inconvenience the majority of the staff. The first goal is to avoid making your meeting a **chore** everyone dreads.

The ultimate goal is that your staff will actually look forward to these monthly meetings. I've a found a basic formula that successfully accomplishes this for most organizations.

First, make one person responsible for facilitating the meeting. This person should take roll, ask everyone to be seated, call on various participants in order, help with handouts or audio/visual needs and wrap the meeting up by thanking everyone for attending. This person may or may not have material to present during the meeting, but it's important one person know who's presenting in order to arrange a logical flow for meeting content. You can rotate facilitating the meeting to include those who may not otherwise participate. Employees might welcome this chance to add public speaking and the ability to lead meetings to their list of skills.

Next, it's always nice if the highest-ranking management person in attendance gives a "State of the Union" address. Nothing formal that requires a speechwriter and teleprompter, just a few words about the accomplishments of the past month and what lies ahead. This may be the launch of "exciting new products," construction news or even updates on annual profit sharing contributions. Remember, it's just a few words! Keep it brief, but give employees tidbits that will keep them excited about the company and possibilities that lie ahead.

If new people have joined your team since your last sales meeting, this is a great time to introduce them to co-workers and make them feel welcome.

Everyone has "housekeeping", a laundry list of information that must be shared, from changes in procedures to new samples and inventory status – whatever needs to be covered with the group as a whole. It's a good idea to print these points on a "Meeting Bullets" sheet and include the handouts in each salesperson's or store's meeting materials.

To insure everyone pays attention and doesn't get distracted by reading ahead, we minimized handouts during the meeting. Instead, we created a packet for each store (it could also be for each salesperson, depending on your situation) with hard copies of the materials covered in the meeting to take back to their locations. Sometimes, we wouldn't even go into something in-depth at a meeting, but instead would tell employees, for instance, that the latest inventory status report or list of new samples was included in their store packets.

Again, try to keep the housekeeping brief and

upbeat, if possible. Sales meetings are not a public flogging venue. You can certainly point out widespread problems, as long as you present solutions or invite staff to submit solutions via email later.

Try phrases like: "We are having a problem with . . . . We would like your thoughts on how we might solve this. Email xyz with your ideas and suggestions." Or "As you know, we have a problem with . . . In an effort to eliminate this problem, we are going to try xyz. Let us know if this makes a difference, or if you see other ways to improve the situation."

Meetings are also good venues for training or guest speakers. Again, keep it positive, motivational and upbeat. Most companies hold their sales meetings in the morning and in retail, usually on Saturday mornings. The sales staff should leave energized, not beaten down.

Always save the best for last. End your meetings with "Fun and Games." Hand out awards and give recognition. Circulate comment cards to let them know how much customers appreciated their extra efforts. Run through the room handing out $5 bills for good shopping reports. Read the names of Peak Performers for the month and give out prizes. Also, announce the contest and prizes for next month, even if you sent it via email so they had it on the first of the month.

Don't forget to let salespeople know who their

delivery team members of the month are and visa versa. It's important to build and maintain a cohesive team. Also, remind them to visit the website or look in the newsletter for this month's winners. (You did remember to have that updated promptly, didn't you?)

This is also a good time to hand out bonuses. I am a big believer in separating these financial incentives into separate checks to hand out at meetings, even if this requires a special check run by your payroll department or service. While salaries are "confidential," bonuses are generally available to all sales staff equally, based on pre-established criteria. There is no reason for results to be secret. Nothing is more motivating to a professional salesperson than hearing about the extra money others earned.

We read off amounts of individual bonuses, team bonuses and special product sales bonuses and hand salespeople their checks during the meeting. Remember, checks and prizes are even more distracting than handouts! Wait until the **end** of the meeting to hand out loot, or you'll have a hard time holding everyone's attention.

Wrap up meetings by thanking everyone for attending. Congratulate all monthly contest winners, remind them to pick up their packets on the way out and tell them to have a great day!

Employ these methods and you should have successful meetings that everyone looks forward to. You'll also see some great sales results from your newly revitalized sales team.

Including the rest of your team

Okay, that takes care of your salespeople, but what about your office, warehouse or delivery staff? With delivery teams, we followed the same formula we did with sales. We gave them updates on "affairs of state," reviewed goals and results from the previous month and set goals for the current month. Then we addressed "housekeeping" issues and offered training tips to make their jobs easier or more efficient. Lastly, we handed out comment cards and follow-up telephone survey results that favorably mentioned the delivery experience and gave recognition for Driver and Assistant of the Month.

We followed much of the same routine for our office and warehouse staff. The idea is to keep meetings from feeling like drudgery for your staff. Meetings are important for keeping everyone informed and focused on common goals, but that's more easily accomplished in a fun and interesting environment.

Keeping the spark alive

Some companies go to great lengths to add spark

to meetings. One I know of had a problem with the staff straggling and dragging in for weekly staff meetings. The two managers responsible for the meetings turned to guerilla tactics – literally! The staff arrived at the next meeting to find them both wearing guerilla masks! Another time, everyone found party hats and horns on their chairs. At yet another, the chairs were on top of the tables! Soon, people didn't know what to expect when they walked in the conference room, but they certainly rushed to be there first! The managers solved the tardiness problem by giving employees something they couldn't wait to see!

It doesn't have to be as radical as guerilla masks. You could also use great little books full of wit and wisdom to provide a "quote for the day" that ties into the overall meeting message. Companies offer catalogs of motivational items with inspiring quotations on mugs, pens, buttons, notepads, as well as other useful tools that communicate goals.

Take the simple book, "Celebrate Today," by John Kremer. This book lists all the little-known holidays for each day of the year, such as "National Goof Off Day" and a commemoration of the inventor of the flush toilet. You can use these humorous tidbits as themes for your meetings, or for a chuckle to adjourn the group. Add a few similar "reference books" to your office library shelves, and consult them from time to time for ideas.

Meetings with a mission

One CEO I know wanted staff members to open up about problems in their areas so the group could brainstorm solutions. She found most department heads reluctant to admit they had problems. They didn't want to reveal "weakness" in front of their peers. She wanted to create an environment where it was okay to speak up, and where everyone viewed meetings as an opportunity to receive help, not ridicule.

At her next meeting, she came armed with a dozen $10 gift certificates to a nearby restaurant staff often frequented for lunch. When the first person spoke about a problem he was having, she immediately thanked him for clearly wanting to improve the overall productivity of his department, then added, "Let me buy you lunch," handing him a gift certificate.

Yes, handing out loot during meetings is distracting, but in this case, it was a good thing. It distracted managers from "covering their backsides" and opened up the meeting for discussions they needed to have to move their company to the next level. It wasn't something she needed to continue, but it was effective for breaking the ice and starting the flow.

Take a look at the meetings on your calendar in the next month. Do you have too many? Is everyone spending so much time in meetings that they have no time to actually "do" anything? If so, improve morale in your company immediately by sending out an email announcing you will decrease the number or length of meetings.

Then think about the next meeting on your schedule. Based on historical reference, will it follow the formula outlined here? If not, can you change it? Have your meetings become stale and routine? If so, they probably could be more effective. What can you do to put some spark in your next meeting?

Remember the goal for everything we do is to create a high performance team that naturally delivers excellent customer service and frightens competitors from your door!

You've probably already realized this is not just fun and games. These are serious tactics you should utilize every day to increase the performance of every member of your team. Recognition not only rewards your service standard, but also encourages others to excel. You've likely thought of other ways to improve the effectiveness of both your contests and meetings. In the process, you've also learned secrets for developing loyalty and reducing costly staff turnover.

Actually, your recognition program will solve problems. The problem may be lack of productivity, low morale, or high turnover, but the solution is to improve these areas through recognition.

The two other top employee motivators are equally strong problem-solving methods. Now we're ready to explore number *two* on the list.

CHAPTER SIX

Leaving Your Mark

Most of us accept we will not cure cancer, negotiate a peace accord or change history in the course of doing our jobs. Still, people want to know the hours spent at work are not wasted; that what we do has value and that we are valued. Perhaps that is why the number two consistently rated item, as a top motivator is *contribution*.

We often say our receptionists are critical members of our public relations teams, but do our actions back that up? Some believe the president of the company should interview the receptionist, not only to insure this person will represent the company well, but also to let him or her know how important the job is.

The same is true for every member of your staff. Besides sales, there may not be an effective way to track employee contributions to bottom line results, but if we didn't need these folks, we wouldn't hire them. That means you should find ways to express appreciation for their contributions.

Think about it – although you know your spouse loves you because he or she married you and stays married to you, it's still nice to hear. It's even nicer to see in the many little actions that speak louder than words, "I appreciate you and I'm glad you're part of my life." The same is true for employees, who often give as many hours to their companies as they do to their families.

Individuals often don't understand the vital role they play in the company's success. They might just see themselves as a clerk. It's our job as leaders (Company Cheerleaders) to help employees recognize the importance of their contributions.

Little things mean a lot

You can demonstrate you appreciate and value them through small, token gestures. I left juvenile valentine cards and small candy hearts on the desks of the office staff, mini Easter baskets with treats, even Halloween goodie bags. Each store also received these unexpected holiday treats for the staff to share, along with a silly card. The delivery and warehouse teams arrived at work to find a giant basket of treats or a plastic pumpkin filled with goodies, along with a note telling them they were appreciated.

Attendance problems usually diminish once employees feel valued. One company instituted

"Welcome Back Mondays," with baked goods awaiting their arrival on Monday mornings. Just a little way to say, "We're glad you're here."

A friend of mine loves games of chance, so they play poker at his company. Every morning, office staff draws a card from a standard 52-card deck as they arrive at work. By the end of the week, whoever has the best poker hand wins a gift certificate for lunch. The game reinforces the importance of daily attendance.

If you have a sales force and regularly do sales contests, it's easy for resentment to build in the office staff. While the office staff's contributions are harder to measure for contests or bonuses, no one discounts their importance. You may not be able to measure telephones answered or bills paid, but it's pretty obvious when these important tasks are **not** done.

Early in our company's history I instituted "Girls' Night Out." It wasn't meant to be exclusive or sexist, it just so happened in the beginning, our small office staff was all female. Even after men joined the office staff, the event remained "Girls' Night Out," though I did offer to change it. The guys said they didn't mind. In fact, they had a lot of fun with it.

"Girls' Night Out" was our way of showing appreciation for the jobs the office staff did every day. Once a quarter, I planned an event. Sometimes

I got theater tickets and made dinner reservations and we had a night out downtown. Another time, we rode a scenic train that serves brunch and visits local wineries. Think of it as National Office Professionals Day, but more often.

These do not have to be stuffy, formal events. While working as a temp just out of high school, I was assigned to a chicken fast-food restaurant chain's regional distribution office. While I was there, the manager rolled a barbeque grill into the parking lot one sunny Friday afternoon, and fixed lunch for his staff.

Though I was only there long enough to attend one of these impromptu picnics, the staff's reaction and camaraderie made a lasting impression on me. It is also why I still eat at KFC today. A good lesson to remember – your internal customers are also future external customers, and can remain company ambassadors long after they leave your employ. Sometimes they even write books and mention you favorably.

The CEO of a computer software company rented an ice cream cart, donned the hat and apron and spent a hot Midwestern afternoon serving ice cream to his office staff. Your appreciation doesn't even have to be that well planned. Once I was returning to the office on a sunny afternoon and called in to take ice cream orders. I walked in with scoops of ice cream for the entire office staff and we all took a well-deserved break. A small gesture, but one mentioned during the employee interviews conducted for the "Best Place to Work in Washington" award.

The same zoo fund raising event where I purchased the scavenger hunt for a sales contest also offers an Elephant Wash. Eight people are served brunch on zoo grounds, and then grab buckets, hoses and brushes to wash an elephant. Imagine your office staff in company shirts and jeans hosing down an elephant! Make sure you have a photographer to capture every memorable moment! The point is to recognize your employees' contributions by contributing to the quality of their lives. It really is about much more than a paycheck.

Some of our vendors routinely thanked our office staff with treats brought in by their sales representatives. One vendor even hosted an annual lunch in appreciation for their ongoing efforts.

Recognizing employees for their contributions to the daily success of your company builds loyalty and reduces turnover. We gathered nominees for Employee of the Month from various departments to insure we recognized contributions that may have gone unrecognized at the executive level.

Seeking those contributions can also solve problems and improve customer service. A common employee complaint about "management" is that it hands down policies and rules from an "ivory tower" with little idea of what it's like to do jobs as "workers."

The net result of such sentiments is that rules and policies are either disregarded or blindly followed to the letter, at the expense of customers and customer service. The reality is that rules and policies are generally enacted to solve problems. However, just as we learned our role is not "firefighter," we need to learn it is not "Mr./Ms. Fix-It" either!

Ask the experts

You can tap into your employees' "sense of contribution" to solve problems. People who do jobs on a daily basis have better perspectives on improvements than members of management who see symptoms, rather than true roots of situations.

In an earlier chapter we discussed Thank You/Comment Reply Cards and how they yield positive feedback. At that time, I mentioned the cards were also a way to occasionally discover problems needing attention. One problem we learned of this way was that delivery crews occasionally tracked dirt into customers' homes. Often cards raved about everything else, but closed by wishing the crew hadn't tracked in dirt. Other customers were livid and literally said they wouldn't recommend us because of the dirt tracking.

Needless to say, each customer was contacted, carpets were cleaned and customers ultimately satisfied. However, I had become accustomed to not needing my "fire-extinguisher," and I quickly grew tired of offering apologies and repairing good will, as well as the expense of cleaning carpets.

We already handed out praise and recognition to our delivery members, as well as our sales and office staffs. That made tackling the problem easier because no one dismissed it with "customers are always complaining about *something*," or worse, "we never do anything right, so who cares?" Instead, the concern was a stark contrast to what they were accustomed to, so everyone quickly paid attention.

The way a problem is broached can significantly impact how quickly and easily it's resolved. In this case, we called a special meeting of the delivery team. A "special meeting" creates importance if used judiciously.

Opening line: "I have a problem and I need your help." That line instantly taps into the part of human nature that wants to help, to in fact make a *contribution*. It also doesn't point fingers and trigger defensive barriers.

So the response was actually audible. "What can we do?" drivers asked. After acknowledging the challenging job they have, making thousands of deliveries into every type and style of home imaginable, I laid the stack of apology letters and carpet bills on the table. "But what's the deal with all the dirt tracked into people's homes? Do customers not have doormats?"

Okay, so we gave them an easy out and let them blame the customer. Some of them jumped on it, saying "Yeah, they go in and out through the garage door and they don't even have a mat at their front door." A chorus of agreements indicated this was indeed at least part of the problem.

"So what can we do about it?" I asked. You see, your role it not to fix it, it's to enable *them* to fix it.

Someone offered the suggestion that we equip delivery trucks with carpet mats, like the stores have by the front doors. Drivers could keep them rolled up in the back, and pull them out when servicing homes without mats.

Since everything in your business is marketing, if you're going to "roll out a carpet" at your customer's front door, what color should it be? If you answered, "Red," go to the head of the class.

Next, I asked what is perhaps the most critical question. "Is that going to solve the problem?" I then heard hemming and hawing, so I knew we weren't at the root of the problem. "What else is causing the problem?" I asked.

Finally, a big driver in the back of the room

stood up, pulled off his shoe and held it over his head. "I'll tell you what the problem is," he said. " It's the tread on these tennis shoes. You can wipe your feet all day long on that mat out in front and the stuff stays stuck in there. Next thing you know, you're all the way down the hall on that off-white master bedroom carpet, then plop, there it is."

If you want the real root of a problem, ask the people who do the job everyday. Odds are they know, but no one asks them for solutions and they probably don't realize the greater ramifications.

"So what can we do about it?" I asked. (That's real leadership at work, ask questions and then shut up.)

Ideas were tossed out and then finally, someone said, "What about the covers people wear over their shoes in hospital operating rooms?" With another round of assent, it was clear we were onto something.

"What do you think?" I asked. "You want to give that a try?" Well, of course they hate being in meetings, so they'll agree to just about anything to get out of there. So I ended with, "Thanks a lot, hopefully this will make all our jobs a little easier."

Getting suggestions for potential solutions to problems is only half the task. The other part is acting on solutions quickly, while the discussion is still fresh in employees' minds and they're willing to try a new procedure.

Our receptionist called the company we order

store mats from and had red carpets delivered to our office by the end of the day, one for each truck. We later ordered red ones with our logo on them (marketing, marketing, marketing!) but for the initial test, we went with quick, low-cost stock red carpets.

Next, we called local medical supply companies. We found one only a few blocks away who sold us a box of surgical shoe covers for a few dollars of petty cash.

Notice, we did NOT requisition purchasing. We did not seek competitive bids. We just went for a small, quick, in-stock option to test the idea. If it worked, we would go through the "normal" channels to make these new items part of our regular purchases.

The next morning, delivery crews arrived to find red carpets rolled up next to their loads and surgical booties to use when entering customers' homes. Since everyone agreed to try these solutions just 18 hours earlier, they now had an obligation to follow through.

I was still in my office that evening when one of our veteran drivers returned to the warehouse. He came into my office, dropped into a chair and said, "Ask me about my day."

Not really sure I wanted to hear, I asked anyway, "So Larry, tell me about your day."

"I got out of the truck at my first stop. I had my

briefcase of tools, my business cards, this rolled up red carpet under my arm and these booties sticking out of my back pocket. Geez, did I feel like a first class dweeb! But I said to myself, 'this was our idea, we agreed to try it, and I'm a team player so here goes.'"

He continued. "I ring the bell and the lady answers. I introduce myself, give her my card, toss out the red carpet and while I'm looking down to put on my booties, I hear her gasp. I didn't know what I had done, but I knew it must be bad. I didn't even want to look. I just kept my head down, got in there, set up the bed as fast as I could, got the old one out of there, grabbed the plastic bag it came in and was on my way out the door. I was this close," he said, gesturing with his fingers to indicate an inch, "to a clean getaway."

"Then she stopped me. She asked me if I'd like milk and cookies. I didn't even know what to say, no one ever offered me a snack before."

"My partner and I got out to the truck and said, 'Hey, let's see what happens at the next house.' It became a game all day. We got kinda flashy in snapping out the red carpet. Then we'd pause for a moment as we put on our booties. It was fun watching the look on the customers' faces. You could tell we caught them by surprise. That was the most fun I've had making deliveries in a long time."

I heard other stories from other delivery teams. One driver accidentally stepped on someone's cat (not injured) and instead of the customer getting after the driver, she apologized, "Fluffy is always under foot." Rumors of unsolicited tips, soft drinks offered and lots of extra thanks abounded.

The delivery team's suggestions eliminated complaints about dirt, as well as the extra cost of carpet cleaning. Not only did these ideas help establish us as the "roll out the red carpet " customer service company, it also made the job more pleasant and easier for delivery crews. It may not have made the physical demands of the job any lighter, but it certainly created better relationships with customers, beginning at the front door.

The extra effort and care delivery teams took to protect customers' homes was immediately reflected in rave reviews on comment cards.

Recently, a local plumber, who's used surgical-type booties over his shoes for years, told me about a funny incident. As he donned his booties at a customer's door, the woman remarked, "Oh, that's what Sleep Country does!" We've managed to "brand" this level of service by delivering it consistently.

Inspect – not expect

So how do you insure consistent delivery of a service? Remember, people do what you inspect –

not necessarily what you expect. While it helps the drivers saw the direct benefit of using the mat and booties, they knew it was expected, as well. Just as we used comment cards and mystery shoppers for the stores, we had a person call to follow up on deliveries as well.

The questions we asked were no mystery. They related directly to the areas where customers said they want us to focus: timeliness, cleanliness and courtesy. And yes, we asked if they used the mat and booties while making the delivery. The answers to these brief questions established the Driver and Assistant's "Customer Satisfaction Score." A five was perfect.

When we started the calls, a perfect five was rare. Yet every night, we required a person to call as many of the previous day's deliveries as they could reach to ask our five basic questions. Each morning, delivery teams found call results posted on the locker room wall. In each meeting, we talked about progress in improving Customer Satisfaction Scores.

Little by little, averages crept up. Slowly but surely, over several months, a number of individuals made their way to perfect five scores. Considering a truck can make up to 18 deliveries a day for an average of 22 delivery days per month, that can mean close to 400 deliveries each month. Nearly 400 homes with narrow hallways, tight staircases, low-hanging trees, and pets and children underfoot, with people delivering a thing so large and heavy most of us don't even want to flip and rotate it every month!

We didn't reach all 400, but we talked to a representative sample – usually about 30%. How many of us would receive "perfect fives" from more than 100 of our customers every single month? What are the odds of avoiding the occasional curmudgeon who hates everyone or just can't stand to say anything was perfect?

Yet month after month, most of our delivery crew did just that, receiving perfect fives from customer after customer. That was our service standard and key element (along with safety and attendance) for determining Driver and Assistant Driver of the Month, as well as giving annual awards.

The unexpected delivery touch also earned us more customers through referrals. Drivers can point to cul-de-sacs on their routes where they've delivered to every single house. That's word of mouth advertising at work. And I know the delivery teams' stellar service played a critical role.

It also earned raves from one very unexpected customer. We compete aggressively with the major department store in our area. While we have sold beds to a number of their employees over the years, I was still caught by surprise when I met a key executive in the company. He actually rushed up to me at an industry conference to tell me this story.

He described a delivery horror story about getting a piece of furniture from his own company. Then he stunned me by saying; "Now let me tell you about getting my mattress delivered from you." He proceeded to sing praises of our clean, uniformed, professional, courteous delivery team with its red carpet and booties. A growing number of curious passerbies were also caught up in the enthusiasm of his storytelling.

I told that story to the delivery crews and let them know how proud I was of them. I also shared the story with sales staff, so they could appreciate the secret weapon their delivery team represented. Every time someone commented to me on a delivery, I passed it on. A local Mercedes dealer told me about buying a mattress from one of our stores. He acknowledged the salesperson's great service, but was *ecstatic* about the delivery process.

During training, I made a point of sharing those very stories with new delivery team members. It's important to help them understand the significant *contribution* they make in the company's success. It was important they understood the history behind some of our practices. Sharing how an idea came about allowed a new group who wasn't there for the birth to share ownership. It also sent a powerful message – that we took suggestions seriously. This encouraged other great ideas, because they knew employees were heard.

This is just one example of how tapping into employees' sense of contribution can be used to solve problems for your business. Like with the delivery crew and tracking dirt, groups closest to them often solve problems most effectively.

When we identified a particular product category that consistently showed a loss, we asked the sales staff to solve the problem. As an incentive, we offered to invest all profits created in this category directly into our profit sharing program. The profits they earned and the contribution we made that year, were significant. And the company still profited by wiping out this significant loss.

Tapping your team's talents

Let's take a look at other ways you can generate and use valuable employee feedback in your organization.

Many retail companies have buyers in central offices who order merchandise for all their stores. I've met great buyers who also regularly visit their stores to see how products are displayed and talk to floor sales staff, getting feedback for future orders.

We didn't need a department of buyers and merchandisers. Instead, we created a "Marketing Committee" to design and select mattress models to

offer in our stores. Our sales team was very knowledgeable about products offered by other stores at
various price points. In addition, every day they
heard about what consumers were looking for, but
not finding, when shopping for new mattresses.
Who better to help merchandise our product line?

We invited the best to participate. A few times a
year, our group of about a half-dozen descended
upon local manufacturing plants of the major
national brands we offered. They tried out all the
models and offered critical input. By the time we finished, we had what our sales staff believed was the
most competitive product line in our market. They
firmly believed we had more to offer the consumer
at every price point – and their sales reflected it.

Not only did Marketing Committee members gain
a sense of "ownership" in the line and the ability to
speak authoritatively to shoppers, they were also our
best salespeople. They not only sold products to
external customers, they sold them to their fellow
sales associates as well. They would come back from
factory meetings so excited about the new products
they'd seen and the competitive situations they now
felt they could conquer. Their energy revitalized the
entire sales force and the results spoke for themselves.

It became an "honor" to participate in the
Marketing Committee. Commissioned sales people,
even people on their scheduled days off, gladly

accepted a token salary in exchange for the opportunity to make a ***contribution.***

Training is another area where your staff can make important contributions. Who better to train new staff members than those who do the job well already? Some of our best sales people served as teachers, covering the areas in which they excelled. One may have been a wizard on specifications, another on the computer and someone else best suited to talk competition. Our peak performers were paid only token salaries for teaching. But they reaped great personal rewards by sharing their talents and seeing the results of their contributions in the performances of new sales people. These opportunities allowed them to develop new skills in teaching, leadership and mentoring.

New delivery people also learned proper techniques from seasoned veterans who routinely earned high scores from customers.

These are just a few examples of ways to both recognize your staff's valuable contributions and solicit employee input to solve problems or improve systems. I know of other companies with activity committees to plan company events, such as picnics, monthly brown bag lunches with guest speakers and even the annual holiday party.

Many companies routinely solicit contributions for newsletters and give story or photo credit in print.

A very successful Texas fabrication company is run almost entirely by teams. It has safety, quality and training teams – teams for virtually every area of the business. Even if you're not ready to run your organization by committee, you can still take advantage of your staff's great ideas to improve safety, quality and your bottom line.

Create a real suggestion box

Suggestion boxes are popular in many organizations. They give employees opportunities to point out problems they might not want to explore publicly. Like any form of communication, suggestion boxes can only be effective if suggestions are sent *and* received. Nothing sends a more negative message to employees than a dust-covered suggestion box everyone knows hasn't been opened in a year!

But a well-tended suggestion box can be very helpful for identifying and solving problems. Put the box in a visible location, but not on the president's door. You want employees to feel comfortable offering their most candid thoughts and they often prefer anonymity.

Show them the box as a group. Encourage everyone to point out problems and offer suggestions for how to solve them. Always give them the option of anonymity.

Tell them when suggestions will be reviewed, the

procedures you will follow and how soon they should expect to receive responses. For example: "We will open the box each Friday and the management team will review suggestions. We'll think about them over the weekend and discuss them Monday. Then, we'll report back to you at the monthly staff meeting." You may even want to post the review schedule on the box itself, as a reminder.

Whatever schedule and procedure you set for reviewing suggestions, be sure it's something you can do consistently. If you want more meaningful suggestions for identifying and solving problems in your business, read them more often. You should read suggestions at least once a month, or it will become clear you asked for input because you thought you "should," not because you value employee contributions.

During the first few months, you may have to send out an email reminder a few days ahead of time that you'll be opening and reviewing suggestions on Fridays. Set deadlines for placing suggestions in the box.

Open the suggestion box and read all of them according to the promised schedule. Try to pick one suggestion to implement immediately. In any event, talk about suggestions regularly in monthly meetings. When problems are identified via the suggestion box, put them on the table for discussion. The group may have solutions to offer, or you can assign a couple of people to brainstorm ideas in-depth after the meeting.

Some companies create contests to see who can produce the greatest cost savings by improving their processes. One auto manufacturer saved money after a line worker suggested workers no longer paint internal part consumers never saw. The net savings was only a fraction of a cent per part, but the company used many of that particular part – enough to add up to a small fortune. The company shared a portion of the annual savings with the employee. As this example shows, employees will offer ideas if they know you value their contributions.

While a physical "suggestion box" may work for a single building operation, many of our companies grow and spread across many facilities, even many states and countries. Local suggestion boxes will still work for problems/suggestions within specific environments, but more accessible mechanisms are needed to accommodate system-wide issues. "Virtual suggestion boxes" can be created, as well. If you already have confidential information posted on the web accessible by password, you can add an employee suggestion form. Your MIS person can show you how senders can remain anonymous. Then you can receive suggestions from everywhere. Incoming mail can often be coded to go automatically to a suggestions folder, where it can be viewed like an actual "box."

You can also post problems on an electronic – or physical – bulletin board and invite solutions. Whatever means you utilize, be sure to give credit where credit is due. If a suggestion was anonymous and you give praise to "whoever's great idea this was," people will probably start taking credit for their suggestions by signing their names.

When an employee suggestion becomes part of your process, be sure to tell new employees where it came from. Make sure they know that idea came from someone just like them and maybe the next great problem-solving *contribution* will be theirs!

A *chance to shine*

Sometimes staff doesn't recognize the contributions they can make to your team or project. Though we each have unique talents, we often take them for granted or don't see other applications. As Cheerleader, one of your jobs is to discover talent in your staff to develop or use in a new way.

I have always been an avid photographer. It was through this interest that a manager in Kansas City first taught me about "working outside my job description." My photography was a hobby and I didn't see any application for it as a secretary in a sales office, beyond decorating my office area. One day, my manager commented on my displayed photos, which I proudly took credit for shooting.

A few months later, he was planning the annual customer golf tournament and asked me to serve as event photographer. He thought customers would enjoy having their pictures taken on the golf course.

I was so proud! Friends always complimented my photos, but this was almost like being hired as a professional photographer! Of course, I still received my secretarial salary, but I was going to get to wear a company shirt, ride around in a golf cart and spend a day doing what I loved – shooting pictures!

The more I thought about it, the more excited I became and the more ideas I came up with to expand on his initial idea. "What if we took advantage of one hour photo developing and customers could actually take their pictures home at the end of the day?" I asked. "Why don't we have multiple prints made of each frame so we don't have to order extras later?" "Why don't we display them when customers come back to the clubhouse that afternoon for dinner and awards?"

My manager loved my enthusiasm for the project and saw customer benefits from each of my suggestions. By tournament day, I enlisted and received approval for all office staff to participate. Some ran film to the mall for developing. Others mounted prints on display boards at the clubhouse, or organized extra prints for easy distribution.

In addition, we all spent a sunny day on the golf course in our company shirts, mingling with customers we often worked with on the telephone. What had previously been a salesperson and customer event became a *company* and customer event. The contributions of the office staff improved efficiency and increased the benefits for both the company and customers.

My personal contribution was widely heralded. So much so, that one of the conditions of approval for my transfer to the Dallas, Texas, office was that I would return, at company expense, to be the golf tournament photographer again next year. A number of next-level managers, whom I would cross paths with in the years ahead, also attended this event. They all remembered my positive role and contribution to the golf tournament.

The experience taught me the value of putting a bit of myself into every job and task. I enjoyed my job more and people noticed the difference. I applaud that wise boss who didn't just see a secretary with a weekend photography hobby, but rather a company goodwill ambassador wielding a camera.

I've often publicly recognized gifted and enlightened managers I've had the good fortune to work under. They often saw my potential before I did, and used their leadership skills to help me discover my own abilities. Each of them led me a little further down the path to where I stand today.

Our staffs consist of unique people with special gifts and talents. It's our responsibility to help them discover their true potential and find ways to use their gifts to benefit our team. And it's our job to create environments that welcome and applaud their ***contributions***.

CHAPTER SEVEN

Welcome Employees Welcome Customers

We no longer live in an era where employees join our companies right out of school and retire 40 years later. Our more mobile society also reflects in employment history. Since relocation no longer requires arduous journeys across hostile territories, people move for a variety of reasons, some as simple as weather. With the exception of employees of a few large corporations with branches throughout the country or world, for most people decisions to relocate mean changing companies.

As an employer, it's unlikely you'll eliminate employee turnover based in geography or family issues. However, the environment we've talked about creating should dramatically reduce turnover by letting employees know they're appreciated and that their contributions are valued.

Many companies attempt to address the turnover issue through rigid non-compete contracts and benefits vesting over extended periods of time. I don't disagree with either practice, but I believe both are "out of sight – out of mind" policies. On a daily basis, these do not encourage employees to stay and make significant contributions to the company's success.

I prefer employees who don't even consider leaving, to those who track their vesting schedules and look for ways around non-compete clauses. Remember, salaries and benefits generally don't lure away employees, even in competitive business environments. In reality, people usually stop looking when they find jobs they enjoy. As a result, they lose track of what they're worth on the open market. They usually put feelers out – to learn if their salary and benefits are comparable – when they become unhappy.

Your goal as a manager or owner, is to create an environment so rewarding, employees don't want to leave. This means building a culture that offers routine recognition, allows everyone to contribute and lastly, makes each team member feel they *belong*.

Before the interview

Rated third on the list of greatest employee motivators is a *sense of belonging*. Creating that feeling for the employee begins during the application/interview process. Managers and business owners commonly make the mistake of not including current employees in the hiring process. No, I don't recommend you make prospective employees run a gauntlet with every member of your staff. There are usually only a few individuals specifically involved in a hiring decision, but the fact the company is hiring should not be kept secret.

Sharing hiring information with your team accomplishes several important things. First, it allows employees to make a contribution. They may, for instance, know someone perfect for the job. Next, it shows the company is on a positive track. New employees are either the result of growth or are added to address problems. Existing team members should welcome both scenarios. Lastly, sharing factual information circumvents the rumor mill. We all fear what we don't understand. If your staff knows why you're hiring, they'll welcome, rather than fear, new arrivals.

Insuring new employees are welcomed, rather than feared starts the day you decide to run an ad or contact an employment agency. You can share this information any number of ways. What is best likely depends on the number of employees you have and whether they are located in one facility or work only one shift. It could be part of your regularly scheduled meeting, sent in an email or posted in a memo. Whatever works best for your group, just start the not-yet-hired, new employee off right by sharing the news in a positive manner with your existing staff.

"Great news!" you might announce. "We're still growing. We need to hire another person to handle the increased volume. If you know someone you feel would make a great addition to our winning team, please let us know. We appreciate your extra efforts to handle the ever-increasing workload and hope this new team member makes your jobs easier."

After a positive announcement like that, employees will probably be welcoming rather than fearful. The announcement contained no criticism of the existing team – quite the opposite. The new team member was positioned as coming to make their lives easier, not to take their places. Even if your ultimate goal really is to replace weaker members, this tactic will reduce resistance to the process.

Now you're in a position to make the best possible impression on the prospective employees you'll invite to interview. Encourage your staff to view applicants as visiting dignitaries.

Give them opportunities to contribute by asking them to find ways to make your company appealing to prospective employees. Is parking challenging at your building? Can you dedicate a few spots near the door and label them with temporary signs for applicants? Does your building have multiple doors, making it confusing for first-time visitors to find the right entry? Simple, temporary signage generated on a personal computer can solve some of this frustration for prospective employees and subtly make them feel welcome.

Take an outsiders look at your lobby or reception area. Are the magazines out-of-date and dog-eared? Do they relate to your business? If not, should they even be there? This isn't a doctor's office, where you're trying to distract visitors while they wait. Are there articles about your business on the walls or in easy-to-view scrapbooks? Perhaps you could put out a photo album of company events, such as the summer picnic or annual awards banquets. The applicant probably won't recognize people in the photos, but an album will send yet another subtle message that this is a fun and inviting place to work.

Remember, as leader, you are not the task performer. Enlist staffers with keen eyes or creative flair to execute these projects. They'll welcome the chance to make a contribution and do something outside their normal routines.

The welcome wagon

Remember when we talked about the importance of involving your receptionist in the hiring process, giving you candid feedback on applicants' "pre-interview" behaviors? Encourage your receptionist to make applicants feel welcome, as well. This could be as simple as indicating where they can hang their coat or offering a beverage.

Once you've chosen a candidate, again – share this information with your staff. "Great news!" you can tell them. "We found someone we feel will make a great contribution to the team. Ms. XYZ recently moved here from Chicago, where she spent the past eight years with a very successful company in a related industry. She'll start next Monday. We'd appreciate anything you can do to make her feel welcome and help her transition."

These little bios also work well in company newsletters and on websites. Some companies even take pictures of the new employees to be included with the bio in the newsletter.

Again, you've included everyone, even those who work in different departments. Now, when they meet in the lunchroom or mailroom, the new employee will likely be greeted with, "You must be Ms. XYZ. I've heard nice things about you."

The first day

Recognizing how important the first few days can be in the life of a new hire, the CEO of a successful software company personally calls each new employee to welcome them to the company. The new employee also receives gifts each day of the first week ranging from flowers to company logo shirts. New salespeople are also flown *first class* to the company headquarters in Minneapolis for orientation and training. This clearly sends a welcoming message to a new employee and helps assure them that they have made a wise career decision in joining the company.

I realize a lot of small business can't afford all *those* perks, but surely anyone has a few moments to make a welcoming telephone call. There are also catalogs specializing in business greeting cards for every occasion including "Welcome to our Company." One of these could be left on the newcomer's desk or even mailed to their home to arrive just before or on their first day.

Does your company have logo coffee mugs? I used to keep a few in my office closet with a couple of logo chocolate bars wrapped in cellophane and tied with red, white and blue curling ribbon. I'd hand them out to visitors from time to time, but that would also make a nice welcome gift on the new hire's desk. If you don't have your own logo mugs and chocolate bars, an inspirational message mug (there are catalogs that sell those as well) filled with candy, wrapped with cellophane and tied with a bow would work as well.

There are countless ways to make new hires feel

welcome and to quickly blend them into your company culture. The genius boss early in my career did something as a lark that proved to be an excellent way to smooth the way for new people. After hiring his first person, his parting comment was, "Oh, and the new person always brings donuts their first day." I raised an eyebrow because I knew this was a new practice.

Nonetheless, I was ready. The day the new employee reported for work, I set out a small folding table and covered it with a plastic party tablecloth I found in one of the lunchroom cupboards. We put the dozen fresh donuts on this table right inside the door to our department, where everyone would have to consciously walk around it to get to their desks.

I don't know about your office, but I find treats usually draw attention. Each arriving team member asked, "Who brought the donuts?" This allowed me to say we had a new person who brought goodies to share with all of us. Human nature took its course from there, and each existing employee, donut in hand, went back to seek out, meet and thank the newest member of the team.

We proved to be such a fast-growing team that soon the sight of donuts on the table inside the door inspired a slightly different question: "Where's the new person?" By the end of his or her first day, the newest member of the team met the others and engaged in the obligatory small talk that accompanies eating treats. Typically, they also received offers of lunch, golf or just "a hand if you need anything." The newest member of the team went home that night not only excited about the new job, but about all their new friends, as well.

Just as people do business with people they like, they also prefer to work with people they like. While it's not essential that everyone on your team be best friends, I think we'd all agree it's better if they at least get along and respect one another. Not only can employee tensions cause turnover, they turn off customers who pick up "bad vibes," even if they can't identify the source. You've likely experienced both cultures. It's no wonder customers gravitate toward businesses where employees are happy and enjoy their work and each other. A natural byproduct is that those same employees create a more pleasant and welcoming environment for the customer, as well.

Birthdays and anniversaries

We all spend as many, sometimes more, hours at work than with our family and friends. Our coworkers become extended families and the simple acknowledgement of a birthday can mean a lot to an employee. I know that the whole "what to do about office birthdays" has become a major headache for a lot of companies. It was easy to buy a cake and card when there were only a few employees. But as a company grows, the celebrations become too frequent, costly and complicated.

Some companies have moved to a once-a-month celebration honoring all the birthdays for that month. There's a cake or cookies during break, a card for each honoree and a group chorus of Happy Birthday. In big offices with a lot of employees, this may be the only viable option.

However, there may be a few minor alterations to make each employee feel a bit more special. In addition to the greeting card passed around for coworkers to sign, another one from the top manager can be mailed to their home. Again, there are catalogs of appropriate business occasion cards where a supply of these can be purchased at a nominal cost.

Have the person with access to personnel records pull cards for each of the monthly birthdays and label each with a sticky note indicating the recipient. In a few minutes, you can sign a month's worth of cards, return them to be stuffed, sealed, stamped and held for mailing to insure timely delivery. In this way, each *individual* is recognized in addition to the group celebration.

Print up a list of each month's birthdays on colorful paper to be posted on your Good News Board.

Only list names, departments or store locations and the date – NOT the year! That enables coworkers to send personal cards, emails or even plan their own celebrations if they feel so inclined. This same information can often be created into a welcome screen employees see when logging onto their computer. Then employees in remote locations see it as well. Ask your system administrator. Both postings serve as wide scale recognition with minor effort, since the task is done just once each month.

I view time with the company as an important landmark to be recognized as well, so include Company Anniversaries in the same postings. List employee name, current department or store and the year they joined the company. Anniversaries cards should signed and mailed along with the birthday cards.

Years ago, a company where I worked had a unique way of addressing employee birthdays. There were only a dozen or so employees and the office manager handled the monthly bulletin board posting and card signing. But instead of one person being responsible for selecting, ordering and picking up celebration treats, the honoree brought in his or her own. It's not as cold as it may sound. On my birthday I brought in my personal favorite, coconut cream pound cake. Someone else brought the makings for ice cream sundaes. A chronic dieter brought in a beautiful fruit and veggie platter. In this way, everyone got exactly what he or she wanted and we all enjoyed the variety.

It's important to recognize personal events such as birthdays, as well as time with the company, to continue to foster a sense of belonging among your employees. Recognizing anniversaries with the company is also an opportunity to thank employees for sticking around – especially in today's high turnover work world.

Team-building

There are many things you can do as a manager to encourage camaraderie among your staff. Teams and committees with specific goals or focuses is one way. This allows you to tap into the desire to contribute and the sense of belonging at the same time.

We found the team approach especially useful for setting up new stores. During the first year alone, Sleep Country USA opened eight stores. A small, but growing company, we called on everyone to lend a hand on big projects. It took us two full days to set the first store but that time steadily decreased as we collectively found a rhythm through repetition.

Once a few stores were open, we couldn't pull all our staff off the sales floors to set a new one. Instead, we invited the store managers to the new "Store Setting Party," as it became known. We met for breakfast near the store (I bought) and then we went to work. Each manager knew what needed to be done and how the finished product should look, so they jumped in and did it. They would grab a partner to help when they needed extra hands, but eventually, each manager developed his or her own specialty.

One would hang the American flags out front; another the in-store signage, someone else stuffed pillows in decorative shams, lamps, shades and bulbs were assembled, while someone else hooked up the computer, phones and sales counter items. I was responsible for draping the divider walls with fabric, silk plant placement and other decorative touches.

Periodically, someone would ask the new store manager's preference on product placement, but miraculously, within only a few hours, it looked like a Sleep Country USA store, all sparkling and open for business.

On more than one occasion, the sales manager and I would pause and just watch the action in awe. "It's amazing, no one is in charge here and yet somehow, it all just gets done," I often remarked. It was more than just the old adage of many hands making light work. This was fun, not drudgery. You could feel managers' excitement, their pride in the company and role in our growth. We opened a new store

or moved one to a better location about 36 times
during my years at Sleep Country, and I loved being
a part of the team each and every time. I've never
witnessed an Amish barn raising, but I believe this is
how it feels.

There are other great ways to use teams to handle special projects within your company. Typically,
smaller groups are easier to coordinate and manage.
Rotate a project, such as the company picnic or holiday party, to allow different people to work together. The new input will help keep the event fresh.
Keep a master folder of information from previous
events to avoid starting from scratch or repeating
mistakes. You could also ask a committee member
from the previous year to serve as leader, giving
them new members to fill the team. This tactic also
keeps tasks rotating, so no one feels burdened year
after year.

Other teams may be ongoing (safety, merchan-
dising community service,), but add new members
monthly or quarterly. Keep in mind; the goal
extends beyond the focus or task of the group. It's
also designed to require people from different stores,
areas or departments to work together; to inject new
ideas into the pool and keep employees from feeling
burdened by special projects.

There are many ways to encourage teams and
many reasons to foster them. Have you ever returned

to a retail store and asked for someone who isn't working that day? Often, the warm greeting you receive from the sales staff evaporates the instant you ask for "Chris." Too often the response the customer receives is "She's not here. She'll be back Friday," with no offer of assistance **today**. Chances are this group of salespeople is paid on commission. While that's not unusual, businesses need to know the customer experience I just described is also common.

Change the sales staff's motivation and you'll change the customer experience. Use team bonuses, rather than individual bonuses. Divide the store's quota equally among the salespeople who work in that store. Don't skew the quota based on experience or past performance. The object is to make everyone responsible for his or her fair share of the store's performance.

This simple motivational change can dramatically affect the sales floor and customer service. Now *every* salesperson is interested in helping *every* customer, regardless of who ultimately writes the order, because no one can earn a bonus alone. The "What's in it for me?" attitude disappears and customers receive service worth talking about.

This may be a good time to mention I don't believe in "split commissions," or salespeople sharing credit for orders that one starts and another finishes. I have seen this end in chaos and bickering requiring a full-time "King Solomon" to mediate. But each salesperson should be able to take a day off; comfortable any customers who come in while they aren't there will receive outstanding service without sacrificing their commissions.

The team mentality requires people to look out for each other, and they can't do that if they're guarding their own paychecks! So I encourage a "no splits – no exceptions" policy to coincide with your team bonus program. Employees will be inspired by their share of the bonus, as well as by knowing it'll all even out when their day off or vacation rolls around and others write orders on their behalf.

Such policies also impress customers. When you order from one waitperson and another refills your water without being asked, and yet another brings your meal the moment its ready, the customer receives the best possible service. I've asked local restaurants where this is the practice if they split or pool tips and consistently, the reply has been, "No, we all serve the restaurant's customers, not just our own."

As a customer, I'm always impressed by businesses where I know commissions or tips are traditional, and yet people who won't receive direct compensation still deliver great service on behalf of both their fellow employees and the company.

Team bonuses inspire other changes too. Suddenly, prima donna salespeople who chide less experienced employees with phrases like, "If that had been my customer, I would have closed the sale," now find themselves needing to *help* others. Your number one salesperson just became your number one trainer, offering tips and personal selling skills to the rest of the team.

Peer pressure is a powerful motivator. Team bonuses put that pressure to work with positive results, creating excellent, well-balanced teams. Staff camaraderie also creates a more pleasant, positive experience for customers.

Think about your own experiences. When you walk into businesses where the staff has "issues" with each other, have you felt the chill? Did you feel unwelcome? Were you uncomfortable lingering?

What about when you go to places where everyone gets along and clearly enjoys one another? Did you feel like you just went to visit friends? Were you comfortable staying and browsing? Did you look forward to returning?

Some of our teams actually created "pet names" for themselves. They even changed the outgoing fax machine headers to read things like "SuperDale," rather than "Silverdale". Once one did this, the others couldn't bear to be outdone and all adopted team names. If that gets confusing at the corporate office, ask each store manager for their "new name," so you can create a cheat sheet, or require them to leave their numeric location code at the start. Just don't make them change it back! This sort of team unity is invaluable. You don't want to discourage team spirit. It's especially dampening when employees are enthusiastic and looking for friendly competition, but are told to "tone down" to comply with unnecessary policies handed down from "corporate."

Creating mentors

Another way to reduce turnover and improve the performances of newer staff members is to assign mentors. You'll want your best people to train new employees, but how do you motivate your veteran staffers to participate?

At Sleep Country, new sales people received fixed salaries during their first month of training, though they spent some of that time on the sales floor with customers. After passing exams in the classroom portion, trainers assigned each salesperson a mentor. Trainees then reported to the mentor's store.

To discourage employee objections against adding more salespeople to the floor, schedule the mentor and trainee on the same shift. Orders written by trainees during this mentoring period are written under mentors' names. Trainees are already on salary. This way, mentors don't lose sales volume while assisting trainees.

The risk is that mentors will not actually "mentor," but will use trainees as stooges, assigning cleaning tasks and odd jobs. Since the goal of mentoring is to bring the new person up-to-speed as soon as possible, it's important for trainees to get face time with customers. To eliminate this risk, we added another dimension to the mentoring bonus plan. Mentors received a 1% bonus based on the volume over goal written by their trainees during the first month they were assigned to their actual stores. This did not reduce commissions earned by former trainees (now full salespeople). This bonus was simply a way to thank mentors for jobs well done.

We awarded bonuses with special checks presented at monthly sales meetings. We also announced the amounts to thank mentors and encourage others to insure the success of those they were assigned to train.

In addition to the obvious benefits of bringing new salespeople up-to-speed sooner, mentoring programs also solve another problem. Typically, people hired and trained together bond. That's especially true of the classroom portion of the training program. However, this is like the blind leading the blind. By assigning seasoned veterans as mentors, you blend new employees into the existing culture, rather than creating a subculture of new people. In addition, the mentor/trainee bond lasts far longer than the training program, and the newer employee always has a more experienced person to call when questions arise.

The end result is a growing sales force in which everyone feels they belong, contribute and are encouraged to excel. That adds up to an unbeatable team, ready to tackle competition or a changing marketplace.

CHAPTER EIGHT

Tackling Competition - Together

Belonging means tackling problems together and working towards common goals. Competition exists for every product, service and company. If you don't have competitors at the moment, just wait, you will! And when you find yourself in a competitive situation, you'll be glad to have a rock solid team.

After September 11, 2001, I heard a news tidbit I found encouraging. In the CIA office, workers hung signs over walkways between their cubicles that read: Saddam Street, Quadfi Quort and Bin Laden Lane. The signs symbolized their **determination** to defeat their common enemies. These were not field agents or operatives; they were office workers. I slept better that night after this glimpse into the depth of their commitment and intensity of their focus.

Every company I've ever been associated with

was known as a fierce competitor. They were legendary, record-breaking performers. Consequently, they were also industry leaders. What I've learned through these work experiences is that knowledge is power. It is essential that everyone know as much as possible about their competitors. That's why we always involved each team member in the information gathering process. They have masqueraded as shoppers in other stores and businesses in order to see competing products, services and systems from a consumer point of view.

You should always scope out new competitors entering your market. Only a fool would ignore interlopers in their territory. While you shouldn't allow such events to catch you off guard, you also shouldn't allow competitors to panic you or your staff.

One of my friends operates a tiny, but very successful, perfume shop. She fretted over the impending arrival of a large, chic, slick, hip store from New York over dinner one night. She feared the new store would steal a significant percentage of her customers.

First, I reassured her by pointing out that each time I visited her shop; I saw a stack of boxes awaiting pickup. A healthy percentage of her business occurred over the telephone and Internet, mailing products to existing customers all over the country. Those customers would most likely never see or hear about the new store in town.

However, I also suggested she prepare for battle by arming herself with information about her new competitor. "Pay a visit to one of their existing stores," I told her. "Linger and observe not only the number of *shoppers* in the store, but the number who actually leave with bags! Some stores attract lots of lookers, but not many buyers."

Then I made my boldest suggestion, "Buy something. Preferably something small." The true measure of a store is how it treats customers with the smallest transactions, not just the large ones. That way, for a modest investment, she could see the entire operation for herself, from product knowledge and presentation, to the checkout process, even the way the item was packaged.

With purchases such as fragrances, each of these factors is extremely important. My friend has always been successful because she understands fragrance purchases aren't about liquid in bottles, but rather the way they make customers *feel*. A beautiful, expensive luxury such as perfume deserves a fabulous, eye-catching presentation so customers walk out of the store feeling special just carrying the bag.

She loves New York City, so she scheduled a trip to visit the flagship store of her soon-to-arrive competitor. I received an excited and relieved telephone call from her when she returned to her hotel.

"Thank you so much! I have nothing to fear

from this new store," she said. She went on to list all the ways her products, staff and services were far superior to the big, chic, hip New York store.

The competitor obviously agreed, because shortly after opening, a team arrived at my friend's shop to make note of what she carried. A few days later, salespeople from the other store called her when a customer in their store wanted a fragrance she carried but they didn't. The competitors sold the customer what they could, and then put their customer on the phone with my friend for the additional purchase.

The next day, my sage friend descended on the competitive store armed with chocolates and business cards for each salesperson. She has seen a healthy increase in business as a result, and now comfortably refers her customers to the other store for items she doesn't offer. Each store earned new customers through this unusual teamwork approach.

A new competitor doesn't have to be a bad thing. Often, more advertisers help raise overall awareness of your products in consumers' minds and generate more sales for everyone. However, while that may be the end result and your story may have the same happy ending as my friend's, you can't afford to wait and see.

Like my friend, you must prepare your team for competitors. If possible, shop the other store. If they're in your market already, have everyone on your team shop them and pool information. Get as many people involved as possible. You'll benefit from different perspectives and they'll each get the opportunity to look the competitors over for themselves. Usually, what we imagine is far more frightening or alluring than reality.

If your team views your competitor as either frightening or alluring, this can be a problem for you. The unfounded belief that the grass is greener with your competitor can result in turnover at a critical time and give the new business an advantage. Also, fear of a new competitor, or even a new situation at an existing competitor, can cause staff to mentally surrender, unintentionally surrendering a portion of your market share.

Information and communication are the keys to thriving in a competitive marketplace. The more you and your team know about the "enemy," the better prepared you'll be to fight for market share.

A good competitor forces you to play your best game. It's often said to improve at a sport; you should play with those a little better than yourself. That forces you to stretch beyond your comfort zone, which is where growth occurs.

Studying your new competitor may expose your own problem areas. But it's better to identify problems early, so you can improve before your problems become advantageous for your competitors.

When we first considered opening a chain of mattress stores in Seattle, there was no shortage of competition. So we shopped them all and discovered weaknesses we could exploit.

When we opened, no other store offered next day delivery, evening or seven-day-a-week delivery. No other store offered to remove old mattress sets for free and recycle them to area charities. No one else offered customers a trial period in which they could test their new beds and exchanges them if they weren't satisfied.

Those services became our signature features – unique selling propositions to offer our customers. Our unprecedented market share proved our strategy a success.

After many years of dominating our home market, a new competitor arrived. We sent our store managers to other cities where we already successfully competed against this challenger. They each spent a weekend in a store – often directly across the street from the competitor. They returned to their stores full of strategies for how to exploit the weaknesses they identified and rallied their teams.

Managers even went so far as to videotape through the windows of one of their stores after hours to show our staff the competitor wasn't new or revolutionary, but merely just an imitation of our stores. By enlisting our team, we improved our business, served our customers better and maintained a healthy bottom line.

As a result, customers who shopped both stores found our sales staff more knowledgeable, helpful and friendly. Our comfort with our products and services was obvious, and this built continued consumer confidence in our company.

The impact of a competitor on your business has as much to do with how you approach the situation as it does with the competitor itself. Teams – like families – who face hardships or challenges together, often emerge stronger and even more successful. Challenging times can bring out the best in all of us and force us to be the best we can be. In the process, we gain a new appreciation for the skills of our coworkers and create powerful bonds. Competition can be beneficial for the growth of an organization. Properly prepared and led, your team will rally to challenges and take your business to a new level of success.

CHAPTER NINE

Reaching Beyond Your Walls – Belonging to Your Community

The sense of belonging you create within your company builds strong teams and improves performance, as well as reduces absenteeism and turnover. However, the need to belong extends beyond careers. Employees gain a sense of belonging from coworkers, family, friends, church, sports teams and the community. Employers should enhance their workers' sense of belonging by encouraging them and giving them opportunities to participate in the larger community.

More and more business leaders are realizing the value of being visible community members too. In addition to the obvious benefits to the community, there are significant benefits for participating businesses, as well.

Whatever business you're in; there's probably a way to get involved with your community that utilizes your strengths and fills a need. For example, large companies often sponsor sporting events, arts programs or other "big budget" events in communities.

But don't let these big ticket sponsorships scare you off. You don't need a major budget or large staff to make a difference and realize the benefits that come from being community-minded.

Even if you work for a big company that sponsors community events at the corporate level, you can still do smaller scale projects within your branch or department. Some businesses actively encourage this. Washington Mutual, a large banking group, provides a community involvement starter kit for each branch to give managers tools to spark local community contribution. Even without formal programs in place, I find it hard to imagine corporations frowning on divisions getting involved with communities on local levels.

Find a cause that fits

The first step is to find a business-community relationship that makes sense for your business. If you sell environmentally friendly products, "Adopt a Highway" programs or local Earth Day Clean Up events might be a good fit. If you're in banking, a community outreach program in which you visit schools and encourage children to save or work with formerly homeless families in shelters on budgeting and money management makes sense.

If you can't make an immediate connection in your mind, bring it up at staff meetings. Tap into the "sense of contribution" to enhance the "sense of belonging."

Our office staffers once asked if they could participate in the annual "Blue Jeans for Babies" program to raise money for birth defects. Since the majority of our office employees were mothers, this issue hit close to home. They were proud to wear stickers indicating they were participants. When asked about the badges while out at lunch, signing for deliveries or running company errands, they felt good about what they were doing to help. And they spread goodwill about our company, which obviously supported their efforts, at the same time.

Other groups participated in charity walks. They built camaraderie, improved their health, raised money for good causes and again, provided outstanding representation of our company as they walked together in their company shirts.

Effective projects do not have to be big, expensive, time-consuming or elaborate. While cleaning out my closet one spring, it occurred to me other women in the office might welcome an excuse to do the same. I received an enthusiastic response when I suggested we run a business clothing drive. One woman contacted the domestic violence agencies we've supplied with mattresses in the past and they agreed to pick up our collection.

On the last day of our collection week, I ordered pizza and sodas for the staff and even invited the shelter directors to join us. The directors not only picked up our donated items, they shared stories about the women who would benefit from our efforts.

I received a number of e-mails, as well as verbal thanks, from the staff after lunch. They all felt they made a difference and had fun doing it. No doubt they'll continue to look for other small ways to have a positive impact on the community, each other and our customers.

Solving problems by helping others

Like any successful relationship, the best business-community relationships are "win-win." I encourage business people to identify problems and explore whether there's a way to partner with local charities for a solution.

Here's a perfect example. We knew when we started Sleep Country USA, that customers typically replace old mattresses with new ones. And they often want their retailer to remove the old mattress. The same is true when consumers purchase new major appliances; they often want the old one removed.

It's become common for retailers to offer removal service, either for free or a nominal charge. With mattresses, the standard practices are to dump truckloads of used mattresses in landfills, or sell them to businesses that recondition, recover and resell them.

Neither option appealed to me. First, trashing mattresses is expensive. There's the cost of dumping at the landfill. Additionally, used beds would have to be stored until enough accumulated to warrant the trip and expense of dumping. Old mattresses would occupy valuable storage space and require labor to handle them several times. In addition, the burden on landfills becomes significant over time. I preferred an environmentally friendly alternative.

The second option certainly eliminated costs; in fact, many resellers purchase old mattresses, making this a minor profit source. However, there are unscrupulous resellers who don't clearly identify products as used and reconditioned, and I wasn't comfortable taking the risk of becoming a supply line for such an operation.

That's when we considered charitable solutions. After many calls to local shelters for battered women and the homeless, we discovered a perfect solution. Our local branch of a major charity not only had the existing network to redistribute used mattresses to those in need; it had the capability to recondition beds that needed work. In addition, we knew the used beds would not be misrepresented to the buying public. Also, we could offer a side benefit to our customers – since we transported mattresses for the charity, we could leave tax receipts with customers who made donations.

This program grew over time, as did our relationship with the St. Vincent de Paul Society. When storing the large number of beds waiting to be recycled became difficult, we purchased a used tractor-trailer to leave on the charity's lot as a storage bin. The charity came to rely on the steady flow of materials, and eventually expanded its manufacturing capabilities, providing jobs for formerly homeless people in its reconditioning factory.

This ongoing program solved a major problem for us, significantly helped the community, provided jobs and minimized the environmental impact, as well.

Previously, one obstacle to purchasing a new mattress set was that consumers felt they had to figure out what to do with old ones. So our advertising agency recommended we incorporate this unique service into our advertising. Over time, customers learned we "recycled old beds for charity" and provided "a tax deductible receipt." In fact, our charity work was often cited on comment cards as the reason customers chose to buy from our stores instead of the competition.

This simple act of partnering with a local charity solved a problem for both of us – we had too many used mattresses from customers and they had too many people in need and not enough mattresses. The program also distinguished us from our competitors.

Many other opportunities to make a difference in our community resulted from this project. A number of area shelters contacted us over the years, seeking mattress donations. The requests eventually required us to establish an annual budget and donation guidelines. They also presented opportunities for our staff to "make a contribution" by serving on the donations committee and gave employees a "sense of belonging" to a team, the company and the community.

Goodwill = good sales

Witnessing the many positive benefits for area charities, the community and our own company, we looked for more ways to get involved. Our multiple locations made our stores ideal drop-off points for collection drives throughout the year.

One of the drives we helped with collected "warm coats for kids." We became a major sponsor for this annual event, in partnership with local radio stations. DJs asked listeners to clean out their closets and donate usable children's coats, gloves, hats and scarves. Our stores were listed as drop-off sites and we placed collection boxes in the front of each store. Our community responded! Not only did people bring in good used items, many brought in brand new coats, as well! Then a local dry cleaner volunteered to clean all the used items.

We collected hundreds of coats to keep needy children warm in winter during the event, which ran several weeks. As store bins filled, trucks that transferred merchandise to and from stores picked the coats up and delivered them to our warehouse until the end of the drive. If you cringed a little at the thought of your office or store stockpiling overwhelming stacks of donated items for a few weeks, relax! It's much easier than you think, and the benefit to the community and your business is well worth any minor inconveniences.

While we didn't establish our many business-charity relationships for personal gain, I have observed tremendous benefits for our business as a result of these relationships over the years.

All local charities have boards and volunteers who loyally support businesses that support them. Like any satisfied customer, these evangelists bring many other consumers to your door. We all recognize the power of word-of- mouth advertising.

In the case of charity drives, like the warm coats for kids, countless people came to our locations to drop off donations – people who otherwise may never have visited our stores. Salespeople, aware of the ongoing community project and needy children it benefited, greeted these new friends warmly and thanked them for their contribution. Comment cards consistently indicated the positive experience made our company seem a more inviting place to shop when they needed to make a purchase.

Some people who never visited our stores before saw items that caused them to consider whether it was time for a new mattress. Maybe, if they woke up the next morning with aches in their backs from their old beds, they returned and made purchases.

I firmly believe every opportunity you have to interact with a potential consumer in a non-selling environment is an opportunity to earn a long-term, loyal customer. Again, comment cards we received reflected this. As many as 25% of our customers cited our community involvement as the reason they chose our company.

Other customers, who perhaps listened to different radio stations, were not aware of the program until they visited our stores. Usually, they asked what the donation bins were for, or salespeople mentioned at some point, "Oh, and we're collecting coats for needy kids if you have anything in the closet you want to get rid of. Feel free to drop them by or give them to the drivers when they make your delivery." In this way, we benefited from the goodwill such projects engender, even among those previously unaware of the drive. The charity also collected a few more coats and a few more children stayed warm.

A community project can improve your image, as well. One year, a small chain of auto repair shops specializing in Japanese autos co-sponsored the coat drive. If you think about it, auto repair is an industry that could benefit from an improved image.

I had an interesting conversation with the repair shop owner at the wrap-up event, where we brought all donated coats together for local charities to pick up.

This was his first business-charity program. When I asked how it went, he replied he initially had concerns. While he felt the project was important to the community, he admitted he also hoped the repeated exposure of his business name on the radio, as listeners were asked to participate, would bring in new customers. He put the collection bins right on the entrance drive, where people pull up to drop off their cars for service. His staff was well informed about the program and whom it would benefit, so employees could answer customer and donor questions. It seemed to me he had done everything to insure the project's success,

"So, were you just not getting many donations at first?" I asked.

"No, we got plenty of donations, but donors just weren't driving Japanese cars," he explained.

Before you get discouraged and throw in the towel, listen to the rest of his story.

"Then," he added, "a couple of weeks into the collection, we started seeing new customers. As a matter of practice, we always ask people how they heard about our business. Almost all said someone they knew made a donation earlier, were treated well and felt good enough to pass on a recommendation."

It seems non-Japanese car owners live next-door to Japanese car owners; they work with them, go to church with them, bowl with them, are involved in school events with them . . . well, you get the picture. The point is, you may not do business with everyone who participates in charitable projects you sponsor, but the goodwill these programs generate will likely return to you in ways you least expect.

The auto repair shop owner also found having the bins clearly visible as people dropped off cars built goodwill. If customers didn't ask about the program, service technicians inquired whether they had useable items to drop off when they returned for their cars. He claimed he could see a noticeable difference in the customers' demeanor before and after those conversations. I suppose people felt more comfortable, even at an auto repair shop, in the hands of a company concerned for less fortunate children in our community.

Besides attracting new customers, we've also found our community-minded reputation attracted new employees. Employees really do want to make a difference, in their jobs and beyond their jobs. People want to belong, in their workplace *and* the community. Employers offering opportunities for involvement in community projects are more attractive to people seeking more than a job and paycheck. And those were certainly the sort of employees I was more comfortable charging with the care and custody of my business reputation.

Maximize off peak times

Throughout the year, we tried to do as many projects as possible in our stores. Coat drives, back-to-school supplies for needy children, blankets for the homeless, and one of our most popular events, holiday gifts for area foster children in December.

Remember, I recommend looking for ways to make community contributions while solving business problems. So, if you're a typical retailer, you might not want to undertake a December project.

December is not the busiest month for mattresses, however. I don't know why, but for some reason, mattresses under the tree just haven't caught on. January however, is huge. Go figure.

While December isn't devoid of business, it's always difficult for retail people, particularly salespeople, to just do okay while his or her friends in other retail stores clean up. It doesn't matter that they might outperform those same friends eleven out of twelve months during the year. The competitiveness of salespeople can work against any retailer at certain times of year, and most of us have some sort of cycle to our businesses.

Since you already know the natural cycle of your particular business, perhaps your "down time" would be a great time to plan a community project. Such a program could occupy staff members' free time and save you from reducing hours or implementing short-term layoffs. Think of the boost to employee morale. After all, this book is about building your business through your staff. By now, you no doubt know I believe how employees feel about your company has a direct impact on its performance.

Even if your off-peak cycle doesn't result in layoffs or reduced hours, slow periods managers view as typical can be alarm to employees. A community project can occupy available time and provide something constructive to focus on. In the end, rather than just surviving these periods of slowly degenerating morale, you can use the down time in your business cycle to rejuvenate employee spirits and company pride.

Here's an example I believe best illustrates this point. Since January is one of our busiest months, we often gear up and add staff in December to allow for proper training. That means we have new sales people, with no prior earnings history, witnessing one of our off-peak periods during their introduction to our company. This could discourage many professional salespeople.

However, in December, we used our stores to collect donated holiday toys for local foster children. Again, we partnered with a large radio station to help raise community awareness and encourage participation. A veteran salesperson later told me this story about his first few December days on the sales floor.

"It was one of my first days working on my own in a store," he remembered, "but no customers came in and I was getting discouraged. To pass time, I called my wife. I even confessed to her I was afraid I'd made a mistake in my new career choice. I knew I was a good salesperson, but you can't sell to customers who aren't there!"

"Just about then, I looked at the front door and saw a family about to come in. I quickly hung up and greeted them. But they weren't customers; they were coming in to make a donation to the holiday gift program for the foster kids. Just as I was thanking them, another couple came in with gifts. Then a mother waited in the car by the door while a little girl carried in a box of gifts that was almost bigger than she was. She told me they sponsored a little girl her age and that she got to do the shopping herself, but that her mom had helped with the wrapping."

"I gave her a candy cane and told her how touched I felt the other girl, who she would never meet, would be. Then, during the next lull, I called my wife back."

"I told her I had indeed picked the right company. Perhaps this wouldn't be the biggest and best holiday our family ever had, but at least our children didn't have to rely on the generosity of strangers for their gifts."

This salesperson became one of the most active participants in the program for many years, often volunteering to pick up overflowing toys at various stores in his personal vehicle. Often, he brought one or more of his family members to lend a hand as well.

After hearing his story, I realized the sense of belonging, so integral to success, goes beyond being part of a team or company. It's about being part of a community, too.

When we allow employees to make a difference in the world around them and give them chances to touch lives, they naturally want to stay. They appreciate these enriching opportunities and, in turn, represent us positively to the world.

CHAPTER TEN

Lead With Your Heart

We've discussed in depth the three greatest motivators of people and how to use them to create business success. However, the underlying secret to making all these theories work is to lead with your heart. If your heart isn't in it, no amount of strategizing will convince your employees you're sincere. And you can't be effective if your employees don't believe you're genuine and that you care!

As I neared the completion of this manuscript, September 11, 2001, happened. Like every other American, I grieved and sat glued to my television. "Real life" suddenly felt so odd I was uncomfortable doing even the simplest of tasks. I found it impossible to focus on the positive message I hoped to offer in these pages. Suddenly, building a business and improving profits seemed trivial.

Then those feelings turned to anger and a resolve to not let outside forces win. I would not allow the acts of a few to rob my life of meaning. I would not let this vicious act erase all the good I've been so fortunate to experience.

I was booked to make a number of speeches to local business groups in the days immediately following the tragedy. When members didn't cancel the events, I knew I needed to honor my commitments to them. Of course, like most of you I'm sure; I struggled to find meaningful words.

One of the meetings was a breakfast. As I mingled with the members, one of them shared this story with me. It seems her friend works in a downtown Seattle high-rise office tower that recently received a bomb threat. On any other day, this would have provided a good excuse to go outside, get ice cream and soak up some late summer sun for an hour. But this was after September 11th. There would be no "any other days" for a long time. Her office evacuated, transferring the phones to the answering system.

Employees returned to the building after getting the "all clear" and began the task of retrieving and returning messages. Before they finished, an executive in another city rang. He had called while everyone was outside and demanded to know why he got the machine in the middle of the day. After hearing the explanation, he replied, "Next time, have someone call me before you just put the phones on answer and leave."

His comment appalled everyone who heard the

story, but I must admit I actually felt sorry for him. Have you ever had a family member, boss or coworker who yelled when scared? I have. I don't believe in my heart this manager was a heartless, money-grubber who cared only about business. I believe his heart stopped when he got the answering machine in the middle of the business day. I bet his first thought was, "Please, don't let this have happened again." He probably had some pretty scary thoughts going through his head until he was actually able to reach someone.

Unfortunately, what was probably in his head and heart did not come through in his words or tone. So the message his employees got was, "I don't care how scared you are, this is a business!" And that unspoken message will damage the business far more in the long run than the hour when customers were not able to make direct contact.

Things would have worked out so much better if he simply led with his heart. Imagine if that telephone conversation went more like this. "Is everything okay? I was concerned when I called and got the answering machine in the middle of the day." After the explanation, if he could have replied, "I'm glad everyone is okay. Do me a favor. Please, if something like this happens again, have someone with a cell phone call me when you're all safe outside so I won't call and worry."

Remember the "genius boss" I've mentioned? Perhaps no one was better at leading with his heart than Garry Coats, my former boss and mentor. I've always worked from his example when leading teams. As you know from previous stories, I started my career as a secretary in an international business forms company sales office.

After working for the company a few years, I transferred to a branch office in Dallas, Texas. Shortly after my arrival, a salesperson named Garry Coats was promoted to Sales Supervisor in a district not performing up to par. In fact, seasoned sales veterans in other districts dubbed this group "Romper Room." The nickname stemmed from the ages of the team members; they were the youngest sales associates. But largely, the name also indicated no one took them seriously because of their performances. The company sent Garry in to change all that.

He accepted the promotion, but insisted I be assigned to his district, as well. He told me this himself, on our first day working together. He took me into his office and closed the door.

"I want you to know why I asked for you," he said. "I asked for you because you've been here before, you've worked for a District Manager and you know the system. I don't have a clue about any of that, but I know what I'm here to do and I'm going to need your help."

"You know the reports that need to be done and when they're due. I'm going to rely on you to handle those things. If there's something you need from me, tell me in time for me to get it to you. If there's something I need to sign, get it ready and I'll sign it. I'm going to have my hands full turning this district around, so I need you to make sure the i's are dotted and the t's are crossed."

"You'll probably see me doing things out there you haven't seen before. If you think I'm screwing up, I want you to pull me in here, close the door and tell me. I may choose to do it anyway, but I don't want to do it in ignorance. I believe it's easier to beg forgiveness than ask permission, so I'm going to keep pushing 'til someone above me says stop. We're going to shake things up and make things happen."

"Oh, and one more thing," he said, pointing to the desk he inherited from his predecessor. "I have no idea what all this stuff is in this desk. I want you to go through it all; clean out whatever I don't need and organize the rest. I've got a lunch appointment. I'll see you in a little while."

At the time, it just seemed like fun. Garry's passion and energy were contagious and I looked forward to the adventure ahead. It wasn't until years later, when I suddenly found myself in a management position, that I realized the genius of what he did.

First, he *recognized* my skills, abilities and

expertise by putting our district's administrative duties in my hands – tasks our superiors would scrutinize for signs of improvement.

Then, he made me a co-conspirator in his plot to turn around a last place team and make it a winner. By enlisting me to "watch his back" and bring up issues of concern, he instantly created an environment where I knew my *contributions* were welcome. I also knew I wasn't "just a secretary." I was a vital *member of the team*.

I should finish this story by telling you Garry did indeed "shake things up and make things happen." He turned the group once known as "Romper Room" into the number one sales district in the entire southern region. People on his team had long, successful company careers. In fact, the company continually promoted employees from this team, including me.

Garry continually allowed me to "work outside my job description" and recognized my efforts beyond our district walls.

Looking back at my career, those days of "secretarial wages" were some of the best times I remember. We worked hard together, ate lunch together, cheered or cursed the Cowboys together, attended each others' weddings, Halloween parties, housewarming parties and even made annual ski trips. Following Garry's lead, I was always treated as a peer and equal, not "just a secretary."

To this day, many of us remain friends; even more of us keep in touch at holidays. Several have spun off to start a company together, and all cheered my own success path.

What Garry Coats did couldn't have been easy. Not the turnaround he executed, nor the vulnerability he willingly showed me on his first day in management. To admit you don't know something is difficult; many have a misconception that once we're dubbed managers, we should be "all-knowing." I've never met anyone who failed because they admitted their shortcomings and relied on their team to shore them up. But I've met plenty who failed by bluffing and bullying their way through, while those around them stood by and watched.

Over the years, when salespeople needed disciplinary action to gain direction, Garry demonstrated the concept of "leading with your heart." He talked frankly with people about changes they needed to make, offered resources and outlined clear timelines. Then, he pulled a copy of a disciplinary action received early in own his career from his drawer.

"I know right now you're wondering if your career here is over, so I want to show you this," he said. "This one is mine, from when I was just about where you are now. Today, we're doing what needs to be done. Where it goes from here, though, is really up to you." Once again, he demonstrated his willingness to be human – and humane – to those in his care.

Thank God, not every crisis we face is of the magnitude of September 11, 2001. Most of the time, our challenges are smaller – turning around teams that aren't performing, opening new markets, fending off competition. But in every situation, it's imperative we surround ourselves with the best possible team to accomplish our goals.

When asked how to get team members back on track in the face of disappointments or devastating loss, I offer this advice. Tell them candidly you feel bad, frustrated and disappointed. Acknowledge the situation has forced you to question many things. But then remind them what they do is important, what the company offers customers is important and what business means to our national and global economy is important.

Talk about the value and meaning in the tasks of everyday life, especially our work. Work is more than just a survival mechanism, providing us with shelter, food and clothing. Rewarding, successful work and being valued by others in the workplace can provide real meaning to our lives, as individuals and as a culture.

Point out to them one of the few ways they can

each fight back against terrorists – or even just business competitors – is to not let them win. By continuing to do our best jobs, run with our most innovative ideas and implement our wisest cost management, we fight those who would take our way of life
from us.

Then, in the face of natural or unnatural disas-
ters, offer your staff ways to help. Maybe you'll
organize donations of money or resources, or make
a group appointment at your local blood bank. It's
human nature to help, to make a contribution, to be
a part of something greater than ourselves.

There may be some business concerns your staff
should never know about, subjects too sensitive to
share. I certainly didn't run through the halls in
those early days of my business, when I wasn't sure
how we'd make payroll, announcing we were
almost out of cash.

However, it's okay to talk frankly about global,
market or business issues where employees could
make a positive impact. To avoid obvious topics of
concern does a disservice to your team. Be it competition, the local economy or a world issue, it's a
12,000-pound elephant in the room. Don't try to
ignore it, hoping no one will notice. Talk about it
with your staff. Keep your cool and don't cause a
panic, but don't try to go it alone. I've given my
teams plenty of tough challenges to overcome. In

every situation, they amazed me with their results.

Recognize the collective strength of your team. Provide employees a sense of purpose and ways to make a difference. Human beings are amazing wells of potential, and in business they're our single greatest assets, our secret weapon against competition. I firmly believe if you take care of your staff, they'll take care of your customers and your bottom line.

The principle motivators: recognition, a sense of contribution and a sense of belonging, can easily be utilized to improve any business. These practices inspire loyalty and help you build a dedicated team ready to face the challenges of an ever-changing marketplace.

Your staff is looking for you to lead. It's essential you **lead with you heart.**

BUSINESS REPLY MAIL
FIRST CLASS MAIL

POSTAGE WILL BE PAID BY ADDRESSEE

SUNNY KOBE COOK, PRESIDENT

SleepCountry
USA

7029 SOUTH 220TH STREET
KENT WA 98032-9802

NO POSTAGE
NECESSARY
IF MAILED
IN THE
UNITED STATES

Thank You

Comments?
Tell Sunny!

Please grade us on the following by darkening the appropriate response:

Level of Satisfaction

	☹ Low 1	2	Avg. 3	4	High 5 ☺

Rate Your Store:

	Low 1	2	Avg. 3	4	High 5
Courteous Service	○	○	○	○	○
Knowledgeable Help	○	○	○	○	○
Product Selection	○	○	○	○	○
Product Quality	○	○	○	○	○
Competitive Prices	○	○	○	○	○
Store Appearance	○	○	○	○	○

If we delivered your purchase, please continue:

	1	2	3	4	5
Driver/Helper Appearance	○	○	○	○	○
Courteous Service	○	○	○	○	○

Would you recommend Sleep Country USA to a friend?

○ Yes   ○ No

Comments/Suggestions: _____
_____
_____

Sales Order # _____ (located top right corner of your receipt)

PLEASE DETACH AND RETURN